An Analytical Study of Words

by
Louis Abbott
(1915-1996)

A Facsimile Project

A facsimile reprint is a photographic duplicate of the original work. We dedicate a large amount of time and resources to acquire and preserve original material, the age and condition of which have a direct effect on the outcome of our reproductions. Like the books on which we base our reprints, our copies may contain imperfections such as printing errors and flaws, as well as user markings, notations and underlining. However, we believe that these works are important enough to make available as part of our dedication in protecting, preserving and promoting valuable historical Scripture study resources. Perhaps not unlike many of the books that we re-typeset, we may not always be in full agreement with their contents.

An Analytical Study
by Louis Abbott (1915-1996)

Facsimile Edition

Nathan H. Pilkington
Facsimile Publication Director

ISBN: 978-1-62904-062-2
of Words
Published by
Bible Student's Press
An imprint of *Pilkington & Sons*
P.O. Box 265
Windber, PA 15963

For information on other Bible study resources,
www.StudyShelf.com

Printed in the United States of America

AN ANALYTICAL STUDY OF WORDS

Introduction

Since the printing of the King James Bible in the year 1611, English Bible translations have departed from the "Authorized Version" in many ways. The English word "Hell," for example no longer finds a valid place in the Old Testament. Most leading English translations no longer justify the Hebrew word "Sheol" to be translated "Hell," "grave," and "pit," as does the King James Version. In the more accurate modern English versions, "Hell" has disappeared from most of the Bible. As a matter of fact, presently, the word only occurs 12 to 14 times in such translations as New International Version (the leading selling Bible) and the New American Standard. Even in the New Testament, words which used to be translated "Hell" are now being replaced with other words which do not conjure up the image of a fiery place of eternal torment.

Scholars are uncovering an image of the Creator much bigger than has been traditionally taught. This book contains the conclusions of some of the greatest Christian minds and why they arrived at those conclusions. This will be helpful to those who seek to enter into their "rest."

About This Book and its Author

Louis Abbott was born in 1915. In 1928, he received Christ. One day, while pastoring a church, a man challenged Louis regarding his teaching about eternal torment. Louis accepted the challenge.

For three years Louis searched the Scriptures, searched the Greek and Hebrew words behind the English words "Hell, "eternal punishment," "everlasting destruction," etc. At the end of those three years, he realized he had been taught error regarding the ultimate fate of mankind. Feeling he could not longer preach the doctrines of his denomination, Louis gave up the pastorate, but he never gave up studying.

Taking Greek courses from Moody, Loyola University, and other places, he finally came to the place where, in order to get further, he had to teach himself. At the present day, his personal library consisting of thousands of Bible references books, probably has more reference books on the New Testament Greek than many Bible Colleges and Seminaries. For almost 50 years now, Louis has been spending many of his evening hours and weekends studying the subject matter of this book. There would be few in the world today who would have spent as much time studying these words as Louis has.

Louis has given me some of the books in his personal library. On the inside cover, he would put the date he finished the book and note the pages on which he made notations. I am amazed at how many reference books he has read. Most people, including scholars usually use these kind of books to look up a subject when needed. They usually do not read these kinds of books from cover to cover making notes along the way. But that is how Louis read many of these very difficult books.

Whether the reader will be given the grace to see the wonderful truths contained in this work, is up to the Holy Spirit. I only want to make it clear in this introduction to Louis Abbott, that the research contained in this book comes from over 50 years of thorough, dedicated years of "searching to see if these things be so." Louis Abbott has come to the conclusions in this book, not because of his religious background, but because he was willing to test his traditions. May the reader be given the grace to put "fear of God" above "fear of man and his traditions" and read this book with an open mind and willing heart.

Gary Amirault, editor

Dedication

There are three destinies taught in Christendom regarding the ultimate judgments of the wicked: Eternal Torment, Extermination, and Universalism. This book is the result of my research on this subject.

I thank the following for reading and editing this book: Nova Richardson, Pat Phillips, Tony Hinkle, and Gary Amirault. Tony Hinkle first put my paper in electronic format. Without this step, this book would not have been printed.

I thank Fay, my wife for her patience all these years while I was studying theology.

I pray this book will be a blessing to all who are struggling with this subject.

--Louis Abbott

Forward

My hope in writing this book, is to conclusively show that there is no valid evidence supporting the translations of the Hebrew word *olam* and the Greek words *aion* and *aionion* with English words expressing unlimited time or eternity. Each of these Hebrew and Greek words expresses a limited period of time, an eon or an age. Furthermore, I want to show that the several Greek and Hebrew words traditionally translated into the single English word "Hell" in many English Bibles, carry no meaning closely resembling the images projected by many of the modern theological schools of thought. While the works of eminent scholars of Scripture, past and present, and those of secular writers will be cited, the final and only authority for determining the meaning of the words rests in their inspired usage by God as recorded in the sacred Scriptures.

Dr. R.A. Torrey wrote, "Usage is always the decisive thing in determining the meanings of words." An examination of the usage of *olam*, *aion* and *aionion* follows. Such a study should clear from our minds the seeming inconsistencies or contradictions in the Scriptures where these words are used.

Much of the confusion resulting in splitting into different denominations stems from mistranslation of a handful of words in some of our commonly used Bibles. While some Christians are satisfied with accepting carte blanche their denomination's doctrinal positions, many Christians are seeking for a purity which can only be found beyond man-made institutions.

One key area various denominations are divided over, is the final destiny of the ungodly, the wicked, the unsaved, the unregenerated or however one wishes to phrase it. There are three views on this subject. Each position claims Scriptural support: (1) eternal torment; (2) eternal destruction; and (3) the ultimate salvation of all. It is obvious that all cannot be correct.

Dr. C. Ryder Smith, a teacher of eschatology for twenty years, says in his book, *The Bible Doctrine of the Hereafter* (p. 258): "In an earlier chapter, it has been shown that the New Testament teaches everlasting punishment. On a review of the whole evidence, therefore, it follows that throughout that book there are two doctrines, which, to the human mind, are irreconcilable: The doctrine of universalism and the doctrine that there are those who will not be saved." The Scriptures do not teach two different destinies for mankind They only seem to do so because of mistranslations. The Scriptures are the inspired words of God and therefore cannot be contradictory.

Another church leader, a professor, author, and doctor in his field, comes to the uncertain conclusion that, to use his words, "Eternal punishment is a half-truth and universal restoration is a half-truth." A study of the words *olam* and *aion* as used by God should dispel such confusion.

May this study help many to become acquainted with the Author of the Scriptures, and to know Him as the Savior of ALL. Truly understanding the meaning of these words should result in one's seeing the harmony of the Scriptures as well as the perfect harmony of the attributes of God with His Love for all mankind. "For God so loved the world ..."

--Louis Abbott

Chapter One

Definitions of *Aion, Aionios*

"Usage is always the decisive thing in determining the meanings of words."

"Over time, words often change meaning, sometimes even taking on an opposite one."

There will be a couple of places in this publication where a long list of references are cited which may be dull reading to some of you. But due to the importance of clearly understanding the meaning of these words, I ask that you bear with me in those two or three places. I want the reader to be absolutely certain that what I am presently in this book has been thoroughly researched.

Dictionaries only give the meaning of a word as it is used at the time the dictionary is written. Over time, words often change meaning, sometimes even taking on an opposite one. The word "let" in the 20th century usually means "to allow." But in King James' England, the word "let" often meant just the opposite- "to restrain." The word "suffer," had the meaning "let" in the 16th century. This meaning has been removed from the modern use of the word. As word meanings change, so will the definitions found in the dictionaries of that time period. "Carriage" was cargo four hundred years ago today it describes the vehicle which carries the "carriage." At one time, a "gazette" was a low value coin which could purchase a newspaper. Today, the meaning of "a certain coin" has disappeared.

A dictionary, unless it contains the etymology of the word, is usually of little to no help in determining the meaning of a word hundreds of years ago. Lexicons, concordances, and etymology books are needed to ascertain the true meaning of a word within a given culture and period of time.

Listed below are the definitions modern dictionaries give to the first set of words we want to look at. Keep in mind ... what they mean today and what they meant two thousand years ago, are two different subjects.

Olam, aion, and *aionion* are defined in dictionaries, lexicons, commentaries, and the like, as follows: (Here is one of those long listed I mentioned)

- Page and Company's ***Business Man's Dictionary and Guide to English***: Eon: A long space of time; cycle; forever; eternally; always; at all times.
- ***New World Dictionary***: Eon: Period of immense duration; an age; endless; for eternity.
- ***Webster's Collegiate Dictionary***: Eon (*n.*): An immeasurable or indefinite period of time; incessantly; synonym of constantly, continuously, always, perpetually, unceasingly, everlastingly, endlessly.

- ***Standard Unabridged Dictionary***: Eon: An age of the universe; an incalculable period, constituting one of the longest conceivable divisions of time; a cosmic or geological cycle; an eternity, or eternity. The present age, or eon, is time; the future age, or eon, is eternity.
- ***Shedd Theological Dictionary*** (vol. II, p. 683): Eonian: pertaining to, or lasting for eons; everlasting; eternal.
- Liddell and Scott's ***Greek-English Lexicon***: Aion: A period of existence; one's lifetime; life; an age; a generation; a long space of time; an age. A space of time clearly defined and marked out; an era, epoch, age, period or dispensation.
- ***Thesaurus Dictionary of the English Language***: Eon: An age of the universe.
- ***Earnest Weekly's Etymological Dictionary of Modern English***: Aeon: Age.
- ***Universal Dictionary***: Aeon: A period of immense duration; an age.
- ***Thayer's Greek-English Lexicon***: Aionios: (1) without beginning or end; that which has been and always will be. (2) without beginning. (3) without end, never to cease, everlasting.
- ***Encyclopedic Dictionary of the Bible***: Eternity: The Bible hardly speaks of eternity in a philosophical sense of infinite duration without beginning or end. The Hebrew word *olam*, which is used alone (Ps. 61:8) or with various prepositions (Gen. 3:22; 13:15, etc.) in contexts where it is traditionally translated "forever," means, in itself, no more than "for an indefinitely long period." Thus, *me-olam* does not mean "from eternity," but "of old" (Gen 6:4, etc.). In the N.T., *aion* is used as the equivalent of *olam*.
- ***The New Testament in Modern Speech***, by Dr. R. F. Weymouth: Eternal: Greek: "aeonion," i.e., "of the ages." Etymologically this adjective, like others similarly formed, does not signify "during," but "belonging to" the aeons or ages.
- ***The Interpreter's Dictionary of the Bible*** (vol. IV, p. 643): Time: The O.T. and the N.T are not acquainted with the conception of eternity as timelessness. The O.T. has not developed a special term for "eternity." The word *aion* originally meant "vital force," "life;" then "age," "lifetime." It is, however, also used generally of a (limited or unlimited) long space of time. The use of the word *aion* is determined very much by the O.T. and the LXX. *Aion* means "long distant uninterrupted time" in the past (Luke 1:10), as well as in the future (John 4:14).
- Ellicott's ***Commentary on the Whole Bible*** (Matt. 25:46): Everlasting punishment-life eternal. The two adjectives represent the same Greek word, *aionios*-it must be admitted (1) that the Greek word which is rendered "eternal" does not, in itself, involve endlessness, but rather, duration, whether through an age or succession of ages, and that it is therefore applied in the N.T. to periods of time that have had both a beginning and ending (Rom. 16:25), where the Greek is "from aeonian times;" our version giving "since the world began." (Comp. 2 Tim. 1:9; Tit. 1:3) -strictly speaking, therefore, the word, as such, apart from its association with any qualifying substantive, implies a vast undefined duration, rather than one in the full sense of the word "infinite."
- ***Triglot Dictionary of Representative Words in Hebrew, Greek and English*** [this dictionary lists the words in this order: English, Greek, Hebrew] (p. 122): Eternal (see age-lasting). (p. 6): English: age-lasting; Greek, *aionios*; Hebrew, *le-olam*.

- ***A Greek-English Lexicon***, by Arndt and Gingrich: (1) *Aion*: time; age; very long time; eternity. (2) A segment of time; age. (3) The world. (4) The *aion* as a person: *aionios*, eternal. 1. Without beginning. 2. Without beginning or end. 3. Without end.
- ***Manual Greek Lexicon of the New Testament***, by Abbott-Smith: *Aion*: A space of time, as a lifetime, generation, period of history, an indefinitely long period-an age, eternity.
- Hasting's ***Dictionary of the New Testament*** (vol. I, p. 542, art. *Christ and the Gospels*): Eternity. There is no word either in the O.T. Hebrew or in the N.T. Greek to express the abstract idea of eternity. (vol. III, p. 369): Eternal, everlasting-nonetheless "eternal" is misleading, inasmuch as it has come in the English to connote the idea of "endlessly existing," and thus to be practically a synonym for "everlasting." But this is not an adequate rendering of *aionios* which varies in meaning with the variations of the noun *aion* from which it comes. (p. 370): The *chronois aionios* moreover, are not to be thought of as stretching backward everlastingly, as it is proved by the *pro chronon aionion* of 2 Tim. 1:9; Tit. 1:2.

Chapter Two

Usage of *Aion*

As can be seen from these examples, some of the dictionaries, lexicons, and commentaries consider such words as eternal, forever, and everlasting to be synonymous to the words age, or eon. In addition to the foregoing, some Bible translations such as the King James Version, use the words "forever," "eternal," everlasting," etc., where a period of time, an age, a limited period, is clearly indicated. Some examples of this are given below. I will give the Greek transliteration first, followed by a literal translation. Before we begin I want to stress a very important point. What follows must be read very slowly and probably several times. I have made it as simple as I possibly can. One does not need to learn Greek to see what I hope will become plain to the average reader, but one does need to go to their translations and to a good concordance to verify that what I am writing is actually in the text. A Greek-English Interlinear would also be helpful, but not necessary. Furthermore, there may be some texts I will deal with that I may not be able to make plain enough what I want to express. If there are some passages you do not understand, just set them aside. I will present enough material that it should be easy for anyone to at least see that these words are not adequately translated in the King James Bible and many others which have followed the King James tradition. With that said, let us begin.

The Greek word *aion* will be translated consistently with the English word "eon," which is but the Anglicized form of the Greek word.

Hebrews 1:2 says: *di hou kai epoiesen tous aionas*, "through Whom also He makes the eons." Notice the Greek word *aionas* is rendered "worlds" in this passage in the KJV. The ASV margin says "ages;" and the New Scofield Bible reads "ages." Ephesians 3:11: "according to the purpose of the eons which He makes in Christ Jesus our Lord."
Both these passages state that God makes the eons; therefore they had a beginning, and so were not "eternal" in the past. Yet the KJV translates the passage at Ephesians 3:11: "According to the eternal purpose which He purposed in Christ Jesus our Lord."
A purpose carries the idea that there is a goal in view, a plan, an aim, a design. Are we to think that God has a purpose He will never accomplish? That is what such a translation implies. God has the wisdom and power to accomplish whatever purpose He has conceived. Notice that in the KJV translation, the Greek word *aionon*, a noun, has been translated as though it were an adjective. That is a serious liberty to be taking with the inspired words of God, aside from using "eternal" where it is clear that limited time is in view.

In Ephesians alone, *aion* has been translated in the KJV the following ways: 1:21, "world;" 2:2, "course [of this world];" 2:7, "ages;" 3:9, "beginning of the world;" 3:11, "eternal;" 3:21, "world without end;" 6:12, "world." This seems to be a strange assortment of English words to represent just one Greek word! As we look at other verses, the confusion even gets worse! Translate *aion* consistently as "age" or "eon" and we do not have this confusion. Notice how *aion*, "eon" and *aionios*, "eonian" are translated in the following: 1 Cor. 2:7 *pro ton aionon* (before the eons), KJV "before the world," New Scofield "ages," ASV margin "age." 2 Timothy 1:9 and Tit. 1:2, *pro chronon aionion* (before times eonian), KJV "before the world began." In these verses (2 Tim. 1:9 and Tit. 1:2) the adjective "eonian" in the Greek text is translated in the KJV as though it were a noun.

Before you go on with this book, please read and re-read this section until you clearly see that the King James Bible and its sister translations have not translated these words properly. *Pro,* in these verses is a preposition which means "before." C*hronon* is a genitive plural of the noun *chronos* which means "time." *Aionion* is a genitive plural adjective of the noun *aion.* Dear reader, please stop and think this section thoroughly through. It may dramatically change your life for the better. The only thing the King James Version got right here was the preposition "before." The translators of the American Standard and the Revised Version, which are revisions of the King James Bible, realized there were problems in the King James Bible with these words. They therefore made a consistent rendering based not upon the Greek, but upon tradition! They translated that verse in Titus 1:2 "before times eternal." Now what is the world is that supposed to mean? How can there be times (plural) before eternity? This is not translation, this is nonsense. But you see, they had to stay true to the tradition of an eternal "hell" in which many people would be "forever" punished. Realizing how ridiculous a literal rendering of this phrase sounded based upon "tradition," the *American Standard* translators put in the margin, "or, long ages ago." Now here is a phrase that makes sense to the Greeks and to the English. Why not put it into the English text, since that is a rendering which is far more true to the Greek and English than "before times eternal?" Tradition!!! It is interesting to note that the *Revised Standard Version* (a revision of the Revision of the *King James Bible*) finally put into the text itself "ages ago," not quite correct, but certainly much closer than its predecessors. The *New American Standard Version*, (a revision of the *American Standard of 1901, an American version of the Revised Version* which is a revision of the *King James Bible)* "long ages ago." It took almost 400 years to break this incorrect "tradition"! They are still dragging their feet in several others places in the English text where they have still translated through the "tradition of the elders," and not according to the Greek text. If it took 400 years for them to come this far with Titus 1:2, referring to a passage which does not touch their "sacred cow," the doctrine of eternal torment in Hell, then how long do you think it will take for them to treat honestly and objectively the other passages we will discuss in this book? We must remember, their very jobs, their very creeds, their very foundation and power of their denominations, that being the fear of "*eternal* torment" is at stake here. Surely, we can expect a fight to the end. "Tradition" has too much to lose in this fight and the heads of the institutions of the church which have been built upon the fear of hell instead of the love of Christ will war with those who demand sound and correct translations to the very end. My dear reader, I repeat: please do not leave this section until you clearly see that the Bibles in the King James tradition are dragging their feet unwilling to handle these two words, *aion* and *aionios* correctly.

These Scriptures show God made the eons (Eph. 3:11 and Heb. 1:2), and that there was a time before the eons, or before eonian times (1 Cor. 2:7; 2 Tim. 1:9; and Tit. 1:2). Since they had a beginning and there was time before they were made, there could not have been "endless" or "eternal" time in the past. When does "eternity" begin?

The Scriptures also speak of the *end* of the eon and *ends* of the eons. Matt. 24:3 reads: *sunteleias tou aionos*, "conclusion of the eon." The KJV here says "end of the world." The ASV has "consummation of the age," telling us of a time when this eon will end, this present wicked eon during which Satan is *theos tou aionos toutou*, "god of this eon." First Corinthians 10:11 tells us of *tele ton aionon*, "consummations of the eons." Here the KJV says "ends of the world;" the ASV "ends of the ages."

The Greek word used here is in the genitive plural, yet the translators of the KJV have changed the plural to a singular word, "world." How many ends can a single world have? Hebrews 9:26, *epi sonteleia ton aionon*, "at the conclusions of the eons." KJV: "in the end of the world;" ASV: "end [margin: consummation] of the ages." So we see the eons cannot be endless in the future, for they will end individually and collectively.
The Greek word for eon is used both in the singular and in the plural in the Scriptures. We are told of the past eons, a present eon, and future eons: Col. 1:26, *apokekrummenon apo ton aionion*, "having been concealed from the eons." KJV: "which has been hid from the ages;" ASV margin: "which has been hid from the ages." So there must be a least two eons past.

Luke 20:34, h*oi huioi tou aionos*, "the sons of this eon." KJV: "the children of this world;" ASV margin: "the sons of this age."

In Matthew 12:32 Jesus said, *oute en touto to aioni oute en to mellonti*, "neither in this eon nor in the impending." KJV: "neither in this world, neither in the world to come;" ASV margin: "neither in this age, nor in that which is to come." (See also Galatians 1:4 and 2 Cor. 4:4.) Matthew speaks of two eons: (1) the present eon, and (2) the impending one. The impending eon is that one in which Christ is to obtain His kingdom and rule for the millennium.

In Ephesians 2:7 Paul writes, *en tois aiosin tois eperchomenois*, "in the on-coming eons." KJV: "in the ages to come;" ASV: "in the ages to come." So there are past eons, a present one, and the coming eons, at least five in all. Included in these eons are all the eonian times that are mentioned in Scripture. The adjective *aionios* comes from the noun *aion* and is defined: "pertaining to or belonging to the eons." It is an axiom of grammar that an adjective derived from a noun cannot mean more than its parent word. It must retain the essential meaning pertaining to the noun. As it has been shown, the noun refers to limited time, which had a beginning and will have an end. The adjective, then, should not be translated by such words as "everlasting" or "eternal." The adjective cannot take on a greater meaning than the noun from which it is derived. For example, hourly, an adjective, pertains to an hour, not to a year.

Chapter Three

The Scholars Speak on Aion

"Even if aion always meant 'eternity,' which is not the case in classic or Hellenistic Greek-aionios could still mean only 'belonging to eternity' and not 'lasting through it.'"

"That the adjective is applied to some things which are "endless" does not, of course, for one moment prove that the word itself meant 'endless;' and to introduce this rendering into many passages would be utterly impossible and absurd."

Dr. R.F. Weymouth, a translator who was adept in Greek, states in ***The New Testament in Modern Speech*** (p. 657), "Eternal, Greek *aeonian*, i.e., of the ages: Etymologically this adjective, like others similarly formed does not signify, "during" but "belonging to" the aeons or ages."

Dr. Marvin Vincent, in his ***Word Studies of the New Testament*** (vol. IV, p. 59): "The adjective *aionios* in like manner carries the idea of time. Neither the noun nor the adjective in themselves carries the sense of "endless" or "everlasting." *Aionios* means enduring through or pertaining to a period of time. Out of the 150 instances in the LXX (Septuagint), four-fifths imply limited duration."

Dr. F.W. Farrar, author of ***The Life of Christ*** and ***The Life and Work of St. Paul***, as well as books about Greek grammar and syntax, writes in ***The Eternal Hope*** (p. 198), "That the adjective is applied to some things which are "endless" does not, of course, for one moment prove that the word itself meant 'endless;' and to introduce this rendering into many passages would be utterly impossible and absurd." In his book, ***Mercy and Judgment***, Dr. Farrar states (p. 378), "Since *aion* meant 'age,' *aionios* means, properly, 'belonging to an age,' or 'age-long,' and anyone who asserts that it must mean 'endless' defends a position which even Augustine practically abandoned twelve centuries ago. Even if *aion* always meant 'eternity,' which is not the case in classic or Hellenistic Greek-*aionios* could still mean only 'belonging to eternity' and not 'lasting through it.'"

Lange's Commentary American Edition (vol. V, p. 48), on Ecclesiastes chapter 1 verse 4, in commenting upon the statement "The earth abideth forever" says, "The preacher, in contending with the universalist, or restorationist, would commit an error, and, it may be, suffer a failure in his argument, should he lay the whole stress of it on the etymological or historical significance of the words, *aion, aionios*, and attempt to prove that, of themselves, they necessarily carry the meaning of endless duration." On page 45 of the same work, Dr. Taylor Lewis says: "The Greek *aiones* and *aiones ton aionon*, the Latin *secula*, and *secula seculorum*, the Old Saxon, or Old English of Wycliffe, *to worldis or worldis* (Heb. XIII 21), or our more modern phrase, for ever and ever, wherever the German *ewig*, was originally a noun denoting age or a vast period, just like the Greek, Latin, and Hebrew words corresponding to it."

The Rev. Bennet, in his ***Olam Hanneshamoth*** (p. 44), says, "The primary nature of *olam* is 'hidden,' and both as to past and future denotes a duration that is unknown." *Olam* is the Hebrew word for the Greek aion.

The ***Parkhurst Lexicon***: "*Olam* (aeon) seems to be used much more for an indefinite than for an infinite time."

Dr. MacKnight: "I must be so candid as to acknowledge that the use of these terms 'forever,' 'eternal,' 'everlasting,' shows that they who understand these words in a limited sense when applied to punishment put no forced interpretation upon them."
Dr. Nigel Turner, in ***Christian Words***, says (p. 457), "All the way through it is never feasible to understand *aionios* as everlasting."

The Pulpit Commentary, vol. 15, p. 485, says, "It is possible that 'aeonian' may denote merely indefinite duration without the connotation of never ending."

The Interpreter's Dictionary of the Bible, vol. 4, p. 643, says, "The O.T. and the N.T. are not acquainted with conception of eternity as timelessness." Page 644: "The O.T. has not developed a special term for eternity." Page 645: "The use of the word *aion* in the N.T. is determined very much by the O.T. and the LXX. *Aion* means long, distant, uninterrupted time. The intensifying plural occurs frequently in the N.T. ...but it adds no new meaning."
Dr. Lammenois, a man adept with languages, states, "In Hebrew and Greek the words rendered 'everlasting' have not this sense. They signify a long duration of time, a period; whence the phrase, during these eternities and beyond."

Chapter Four

Apparent Bible Contradictions

"If it is insisted that aionios means everlasting, this statement is absurd. It is impossible that anything should take place 'before everlasting times.' "

"Sodom and her daughters, shall return to their former estate."

"Endlessness is expressed by such particles as 'not,' 'un-,' 'in-,' '-less.' "

The Scriptures, the ultimate authority for God's use of words, use the adjective *aionios* in the Greek New Testament thus: 2 Timothy 1:9 and Titus 1:2 "*pro chronon aionion,*" "before times eonian." KJV: "before the world began." ASV: "before times eternal." As mentioned previously, since these verses tell of time before the eons, eonian times cannot be "eternal." Eternity has no beginning, so nothing can be *pro*, "before."

The ASV is one of our better translations in the English language. With all due respect to the committee which worked at making that version, let it be said its members missed the meaning of this phrase and translated it with nonsensical terms. Dr. Marvin R. Vincent, in his *Word Studies of the New Testament* (vol. IV, p. 291): "If it is insisted that aionios means everlasting, this statement is absurd. It is impossible that anything should take place 'before everlasting times.'" The phrase "before times eternal" is actually a contradiction in three words. The ASV margin reads: "long ages ago;" a much better translation.

Ezekiel 16:55 says, "When thy sisters, Sodom and her daughters, shall return to their former estate." Since this scripture refers to a restoration of Sodom, its judgment cannot be for "eternity." In Jude, the Greek adjective *aionios*, eonian, is used when the judgment of Sodom is mentioned.

Jude 7 states that Sodom is an example of *puros aioniou dikên hupechousai*, "experiencing the justice of fire eonian." KJV: "suffering the vengeance of eternal fire." In this translation, the KJV at Jude 7 contradicts that of Ezekiel 16:50-56. Those visiting the area today see no fire, for if our archaeologists are correct in locating its former site, it lies beneath a sea. Many such seeming contradictions would not exist in the KJV had the Greek word been translated correctly to express limited time, instead of "eternal." Philemon tells of a runaway slave who was converted by Paul to believing in the risen Christ. This slave was returned to his master, Philemon. Paul writes to Philemon, saying (v. 15), *echoristê pros horan hina aionion auton apechês*, "he was separated for an hour that you may be receiving him as an eonian repayment." The KJV says: "He therefore departed for a season that thou shouldst receive him forever." This translation seems to teach "eternal slavery." Correctly translated, there is no problem.

At Romans 16:25, the ASV reads, "*Now to him that is able to establish you according to my gospel and the preaching of Jesus Christ, according to the revelation of the mystery which has been kept in silence through times eternal.*" If this verse is teaching of a mystery kept in silence through "*times eternal,*" the mystery would never have been made known. The context in which this verse lies shows that aionios, eonian, cannot be referring to "eternal" or "endless" time, for the verse following (v. 26) says: "*but is now manifested.*" If we are to understand "eternal" to refer to unlimited time, then how could the mystery now be manifested? The KJV says, "*which has been kept secret since the world began, but is now manifested.*" The translators recognized that limited time was in view.

The Greek text of this passage reads, "*to de dunameno humas stopixai kata to euagelion mou kai kêrugma iêsou christou kata apokalupsin musteriou chronois aioniois sesigemenou phanerothentos de nun.*" "*Now to Him Who is able to establish you according to my evangel, and the heralding of Jesus Christ, according to the revelation of a secret having been hushed in times eonian, yet manifested now.*" Again, there is no contradiction when the translation is faithful to the Greek text, by simply transliterating the word *aionios* into the English word "eonian." The *world* is not that which is in view here, but *time*.

Many present the argument, "If *aionios*, eonian, does not mean endless time, then the believers do not have eternal, or everlasting life. The word is used at Romans 16:26 concerning God, and surely He is 'eternal;' therefore, the word must mean unlimited." As has been shown, the word in itself refers to limited time. However, the Greek does have a way of expressing endlessness by using words other than eon or eonian, such as in Luke 1:33: *ouk estai telos*, "there will be no end." Endless life is spoken of at Hebrews 7:16 thus: *zoâs akatalutou*, "indissoluble life." The margin of the ASV: "indissoluble life." KJV: "endless life."

Believers do have endless life, for 1 Cor. 15:42 says the dead will be raised in "incorruption," and 1 Cor. 15:53 speaks of "deathlessness," or "immortality" (Greek: *aphtharsia* and *athanasia*) Endlessness is expressed by such particles as "not," "un-," "in-," "-less." Death will ultimately be abolished (see 1 Cor. 15:16), and when death is abolished, all that can remain is endless life for all. First Corinthians 15:22 in its context says that life will be IN CHRIST, where there will be no more dying, and those in the resurrection here mentioned will be incorruptible and immortal (see 1 Cor. 15:42, 53).

Chapter Five

"Forever and Ever" -- A Poor Translation

"If the Greek words eis tous aionas ton aionon mean endless time, as translated in the KJV, 'forever and ever,' we have a contradiction in Scripture."
-Dr. William Barclay

"This view (Restitution of All) is so clearly Scriptural that the only surprise is that it has not been more definitely and widely held."
-Dr. A.T. Pierson

There is no doubt that God has always existed, but the statement at Romans 16:26 speaks of Him as an eonian God. The Scriptures say He made the eons, so He existed before they were made, and He will exist after the eons have been concluded (1 Cor. 10:11; Heb. 9:26). He is endless. To argue that "eonian God" makes the "eonian" unlimited time because God is unlimited is illogical. Isaiah 54:5, KJV, calls Him "the God of the whole earth." This does not preclude Him from also being the God of the entire universe. In the context of Romans 16:26, He is called the "eonian God," but He was God before the eons were made; He is God during all the eons, and in post-eonian times. In other words, just because the Scriptures refer to Him as the "God of the ages" does not preclude Him from being the God of eternity. The Scriptures declare Him the "God of Abraham, Isaac, and Jacob," and "the God of Israel." Does that mean He cannot therefore be the God of the gentiles, of the whole universe? Of course not!

As for the KJV translation, "forever and ever," there are some students of the Greek who admit that this is not a faithful translation of the Greek words found in the text. The Greek uses *three distinct phrases*, all of which are translated the same in the KJV.

Hebrews 1:8: h*o thronos sou ho theos eis ton aiona tou aionos*, "Thy throne, O God, is for the eon of the eon." In both occurrences in this verse, the Greek word we translated "eon" appears in the singular.

Ephesians 3:21: *auto he doxa en te ekklesia kai en Christo Iesou eis pasas tas geneas tou aionos ton aionon*, "To Him be the glory in the ecclesia and in Christ Jesus for all the generations of the eon of the eons. Amen." Here the Greek word for eon is used twice. The first time it is in the singular; the second time it is in the plural.

Galatians 1:5: *ho he doxa eis tous aionas ton aionon*, "To Whom be glory for the eons of the eons." Here the Greek word for eon appears twice in the plural.

Philippians 1:10 says (ASV margin), "so that ye may distinguish the things that differ." Since the words of God are inspired and are used precisely, to ignore the differences in these passages is to ignore what He is saying.

Hebrews 1:8 is a quotation from Psalm 45:6, LXX, where the Greek text says, *eis ton aiona tou* aionos, "into the eon of the eon," - the singular form for eon in both occurrences. The preposition *eis* is translated "into" or "unto;" idiomatically, "for." Bagster's ***Analytical Greek Lexicon and Concordance*** defines it: "*eis*, into, to as far as, to the extent of."

Dr. E.W. Bullinger's ***Lexicon and Concordance*** says (p. 804), "*eis*, unto, when referring to time, denoting either the interval up to a certain point, during; or the point itself as the object or aim of some purpose, up to, for."

Dr. Nigel Turner, in his book, ***Grammatical Insights into the N.T.***, says (p. 91), "*eis* involves a movement for development toward a goal." If *eis* means as far as, to the extent of, or a movement or development toward a goal, then it cannot be used with words meaning endless or unlimited time.

Ephesians 3:21: *eis pasas tas geneas tou aionos ton aionon*, "for all the generations of the eon of the eons." KJV: "throughout all the ages, world without end." ASV margin: "unto all the generations of the age of the ages." Young's Literal Translation: "into the age of the ages." The "eon of the eons" refers to a crowning eon of another which precedes it. So what is meant by this expression? Many KJV tradition scholars say that these three different Greek phrases are idiomatic expressions for "eternity." Idiotic, perhaps, but not idiomatic! Similar expressions used in the Scriptures are cited in order to illustrate the meaning: Song of Solomon 1:1, "song of songs;" Eccl. 12:8, "vanity of vanities;" Gen. 9:25, "servant of servants;" Ex. 26:33, "holy of the holies;" Deut. 10:17, "God of gods and Lord of lords;" Dan. 8:25, "prince of princes;" Phil. 3:5, "Hebrew of Hebrews;" 1 Tim. 6:15, "King of kings and Lord of lords." Most students of the Scriptures understand what is meant by such expressions, so why is Eph. 3:21, "eon of the eons" an enigma? The eon of the eons refers to the final and greatest of all eons. That it cannot refer to "eternity" is shown by the statement that there will be "generations," which implies procreation, which will not happen in eternity since we will then be like the angels. This eon succeeds the millennial eon, and is previous to the final state.

There are others who teach the same. Dr. A.T. Pierson supports this view in his book, ***The Bible and Spiritual Life***: "This view is so clearly scriptural that the only surprise is that it has not been more definitely and widely held. It adds immeasurably, both to the glory of Christ as the coming King, and the Father as the former and framer of the ages. It is the period typified by the eighth day of the Mosaic Code: the perfect glory of Christ, reserved for 'the morrow after.' The millennial 'Sabbath.' And while the millennial period is limited to a thousand years, there are no definite limits to this final age of glory."

Mr. George Saltau, in his book, ***Past, Present and Future***, adopts the same view.

Clarence Larkin, ***Dispensational Truth, or God's Plan and Purpose in the Ages***, shows (p. 3, chart "The Ages") an age succeeding the kingdom age, which he calls the "perfect age." This "perfect age" is also shown in other charts in Mr. Larkin's book.
The expression, "eon of the eons," is not limited to its use at Eph. 3:21. In the LXX at Dan. 7:18 we see, h*eos aionos ton aionon*, "until eon of the eons." In the Song of the Three Children (LXX, Septuagint), at the end of verse 68, there is, *kai eis ton aiona ton aionon*, "and into the eon of the eons." In the book of Enoch there is a similar expression: "until the judgment of the eon of the eons be accomplished."

Windet, in ***De Vita Functor Statu***, states, "However you understand the phrase, it could not be used unless it signified something less than endlessness; for 'completion' does not accord with true endlessness." Therefore, the expression "eon of the eons" and "eon of the eon" mean the last and crowning eon in which Christ will hand everything to His Father, entirely subjected (1 Cor. 15:22-28). We know that the millennial eon will not be one of such complete subjection, for Christ will rule with a rod of iron, and at its close, after the most wonderful and beneficial rule by His sceptre, at the instigation of Satan, loosed from the pit, large numbers of those who have been blessed under Christ's gracious reign will revolt against Him (Rev. 20:7-9). While there may be many different interpretations about this "thousand year period," clearly we have time, and things not yet subjected. This revolt shows that the subjection spoken of at 1 Cor. 15:22-28; Eph. 1:9-11; Phil. 2:10-11; and Col. 1:10-20 has not been completed. It will take yet another eon, following the millennial one, with Christ reigning to end all insubordination in all His realms, before He will finally surrender to His Father all completed, so that the Father can be "all in all." The final eon is that of new heavens and the new earth wherein reigns righteousness (2 Pet. 3:13). That is the one called the "eon of the eon" (Heb. 1:8). It is also called the "eon of the eons" at Eph 3:21, because it is paramount to all preceding eons, including the millennial eon in which Christ Jesus reigns as Messiah and King. Paul writes (Eph. 2:6,7) of the blessings of the coming eons. He says: "And He rouses us together and seats us together among the celestials in Christ Jesus, that in the oncoming eons, He may be displaying the transcendent riches of His grace in His kindness to us in Christ Jesus" (see also Eph. 3:20-21).

Thus, in the coming eons, the millennial and the succeeding eon, Christ Jesus will be displaying His transcending riches to us. We must be careful when talking about what God will do in future generations and ages. For too often we project our own ideas onto the plan of God. I hope I have not crossed that line. Yet when it comes to the correct rendering of these words, I feel certain what you are reading sheds much light which many Bible translations have hidden from us.

Let us get back to "forever and ever." The Greek phrase *eis tous aionas ton aionon*, "for the eons of the eons," occurs about twenty times in the Greek New Testament in this combination. The ASV margin and some other versions, lexicons, dictionaries, and commentaries translate the phrase correctly.

Windet, in ***De Vita Functora Statu***, of 1633 says (p. 170), "*eis tous aionas ton aionon*, of the New Testament meant a finite period."

At 1 Cor. 15:25, where the Greek text shows, *dei gar auton basileuein achri hou thê pantas tous echthrous hupo tous podas autou*, "For He must be reigning until He should be placing all His enemies under His feet." This clearly states that Christ's reigning is limited. There is no Scripture to contradict the statement when *aion* and *aionios* are correctly translated.

Dr. William Barclay concurs in his commentary (p. 166-169) on The Letters to the Corinthians. If the Greek words *eis tous aionas ton aionon* mean endless time, as translated in the KJV, "forever and ever," we have a contradiction in Scripture, for Rev. 11:15 says, in the same version: "*The kingdoms of this world are become the kingdoms of our Lord and His Christ, and He shall reign forever and ever.*" That contradicts 1 Cor. 15:25, which says: "He must be reigning till..." If Rev. 11:15 is translated "eons of the eons," or "ages of the ages," there is no contradiction. The ASV says (1 Cor. 15:24-25), "*Then cometh the end, when He shall deliver up the kingdom to God., even the Father; When He shall have abolished all rule and all authority and power. For He must reign till He hath put all His enemies under His feet;*" consequently, the reigning of Christ Jesus and the saints (Rev. 22:5) will be "for the eons of the eons" or "for the ages of the ages" (see the ASV margin here).

Eis tous aionas is accusative plural, "for the eons," or "for the ages," and these words are not "forever and ever," which are in the singular. The word *ton* is the genitive plural article, and in our syntax should be translated "of the." In this Greek clause, there is no word that means "and," as the Greek conjunction *kai*; "and," is not in this clause. The word *aionon* is the genitive plural of the noun *aion*, and the genitive plural in this syntax should be translated "eons," or "ages;" hence *ton aionon*, "of the eons." Anyone can study these words and see that "forever and ever" is not a good translation of these Greek words. As *eis* is used in this clause and as *eis* involves a movement or development toward a goal, this clause cannot mean endlessness.

As mentioned previously, there are several analogous expressions in the Scriptures which should show the meaning of the words under discussion. In Ex. 26:33 (LXX), *tou hagiou ton hagion*, "in the holy of the holies." This is similar to the "eon of the eons" of Eph. 3:21. In II Kings 8:6 (LXX) we see, *eis ta hagia ton hagion*, "for the holies of the holies"- similar to "eons of the eons." The "holy of the holies" and "holies of the holies" refer to the tabernacle. Psalm 44:7 says, *ho thronos sou ho theos, eis ton aiona tou aionos*, "Thy throne, O God, is for the eon of eon"- similar to Heb. 1:8. Daniel 7:18: "until eon of the eons" and similar to that of Eph. 3:21, where a singular is followed by a plural, "eon of the eons." In these expressions we see the eons corresponding to the holies in the tabernacle. While there are many different teachings on the types in the Tabernacle of Moses, it should not be too difficult to see that there were at least five divisions: (1) without the camp; (2) in the camp; (3) in the court; (4) in the holy place; and (5) in the holy of holies. These may be likened to the five eons we find in the Scriptures (past eons, present eon, future eons). The last eon is called the "eon of the eons," because it, like the "holy of holies," is the climax of the others. In Hebrews chapter 9, the Greek text of Nestle reads (margin v. 25), *eis ta hagia ton hagion*, "into the holies of the holies," and (v. 3), *hagia hagion*, "holies of holies." Just as the two holy places in the tabernacle are called the holies of holies, so the last two eons are often called the eons of the eons. As the tabernacle illustrated man's approach to God, it corresponds closely with the eonian times, which also brings man to God. The "holy of holies" was a single holy place. The "eon of eons," a single eon. It was the pre-eminence of the "holy of holies," in relation to the other holy places, which caused it to be so designated. So the pre-eminence of the "eon of the eons" lies in its being the fruitage and harvest of previous eons. The same is true of the "holies of the holies" of Heb. 9:25. They may be likened to the "eons of the eons" of Rev. 11:15; 22:5. Luke 1:33 says of Christ's "kingdom there shall be no end." While the kingdom itself will not end, but the reign of Christ for the eons of the eons will end when He delivers up the kingdom to the Father (1 Cor. 15:24-26).

Mr. W. Kelly, in his book, ***Lectures on the Book of Revelation***, commenting upon the saints' reign, states (p. 435-436), "Supposing that God's Word speaks of the earthly state of things and uses the expression 'reigning forever and ever,' as in Daniel 7 and Luke 1, it cannot be understood absolutely. The words must be limited by the subject-matter of which God is speaking, so in Daniel 7:27 the kingdom under the whole heaven, which is given to the people of the saints of high places, is said to be an everlasting kingdom. This, I apprehend, is the same period that is called here the thousand years."

The sentence in Rev. 22:5 saying: "They will be reigning for the eons of the eons" shows that the expression has no reference either to the present or to the preceding eons. The Greek verb *basileusousin*, "they will be reigning" is a third-person plural future active indicative form; so this reigning must be future. In this present eon, as in those preceding ones, the slaves, or servants, of God are not reigning. Similarly, that God and Christ are living for "the eons of the eons" (Rev. 1:18; 4:9; 10:6; 15:7) has reference to the eons of the future, not to the present eon. That is not to say that God and Christ Jesus are not living during the previous eons. God was the living pre-eonian God. He is the living eonian God, and He will be the living post-eonian God. Paul, when writing to Timothy, said (1 Tim. 4:10), "For this we are toiling and being reproached, for we rely on the living God, Who is the Saviour of all mankind, especially of believers."

Two scriptures state positively that the eons will end: 1 Cor. 10:11, *tauta de tupikos sunebainen ekeinois egraphê de pros nouthesian hêmon eis hous ta telê ton aionon katêntêken*, "Now those things befalls them typically, yet it was written for our admonition, to whom the consummations of the eons have attained." Paul had said what those things are, which befalls them typically, in the preceding verses. Yet "it was written" is in the singular, for "our" (plural) admonition- the "our" referring to the saints, who are the present believers. "To whom," referring to the saints, "the consummations of the eons have attained." The Corinthian saints had attained the consummations of eons in spirit because they were a new creation (2 Cor. 5:17). Some day all will be a new creation (Rev. 21:5). Now, only the saints who are in Christ are of the new creation, but it is God's goal for the eons to head up all in the Christ, as stated at Eph. 1:9-11. Salvation for **all** is God's plan for the eons. Those saints believing now have attained that purpose, so have attained the consummation of the eons.

While some doubt such an exegesis of 1 Cor. 10:11, others, such as the writer of the ***New Dictionary of the N. T. Theology***, concur (vol. 1, p. 324): "Paul also speaks of a movement from God to man. 1 Corinthians 10:11 speaks of us 'upon whom the end of the ages has come.' Hebrews 9:26 contains a similar expression, 'at the end of the ages' (time, art. *aion*). Christ appeared to put away sin by the sacrifice of Himself. The movement directed by God towards its end; with us it has now attained its goal. The thought also contains the certainty that with Christ, Who inaugurates the end of the ages, a new world era and order of things has begun. Admittedly, this is apparent only to the believer." Consequently, with the saints it is possible in spirit to taste the powers of the ages to come (Heb. 6:5). At Hebrews 9:26 the Greek says, *epei edei auton pollakis pathein apo kataboles kosmou nuni de hapax epi sunteleia ton aionon eis athetêsin tês hamartias dia testhusias autou pephanerotai*, "*Since then, He must often be suffering from the disruption of the world, yet now, once, at the conclusion of the eons, for the repudiation of sin through His sacrifice, He has been manifested.*" In the clause, "He has been manifested," the verb is a third-person singular perfect passive indicative. The Greek perfect tense denotes the present state, resultant upon a past action. There is no English tense which corresponds to that of the Greek perfect, so this form is a difficult one to convey into English. It may be translated: "through His sacrifice, He is manifested." But it is clear His sacrifice was not at the "end of the world," as the KJV says, since the world continues. But it is equally clear that His sacrifice was not at the "conclusion of the eons," since Paul wrote of "this present wicked eon" and the "on-coming eons" (Gal. 1:4; Eph. 2:7). Sin still remains, and there is a world of sinners; but when the eons come to a conclusion, sin will be repudiated by virtue of His sacrifice.

In Romans 4:17 Paul says, "*According as it is written that, a father of many nations I have appointed you, facing which, he believed it of the God Who is vivifying the dead and calling what is not as if it were.*" Here Paul is writing of Abraham, that Abraham believes God. The God Abraham believes is the God "*who is vivifying the dead and calling what is not as if it were.*" God did not say, "I *will* appoint you a father of many nations," but "I *have* appointed you," using a Greek perfect verb, which indicates a completed action with a resultant state of being. As God stated it, it is already an accomplished fact, yet at the time, Abraham did not even have a son, and he was nearly one hundred years old. So God was there calling what was not as though it were. God speaks so of us, when He says: "*Now whom He designates beforehand, these He calls also, and whom He calls, these He justifies also, now whom He justifies, these He glorifies also*" (Rom. 8:29-30; see Eph. 1:3-8). Are we glorified now? Certainly not! But God is following the same pattern of dealing with us as with Abraham, in that He is calling what is not as if it were. God says that He "seats us together in heavenly places in Christ Jesus" (Eph. 2:6), yet we are still in this world, and a part of an ecclesia on the earth. He can make such a statement because He can, and will, do what He says.

Because we are a new creation in Christ Jesus (2 Cor. 5:17), we have attained to the consummations of the eons (1 Cor. 10:11). At the conclusion of the eons, sin will be repudiated. At present God is "calling what is not as if it were." Only God is able to do that.

The Scriptures teach that during the eons mankind is experiencing evil, sin, sickness, death, judgments, generation, opposition from sovereignties, authorities and powers, all of which will be nullified or abolished, as stated in 1 Cor. 15:22-28.

Luke 1:50 says, *kai to eleos autou eis geneas kai geneas tois phoboumenois auton*, "*and His mercy is for generations and generations, for those who are fearing Him.*" In the phrase, "for generations and generations," there is an example of two plural nouns being used with the conjunction *kai*, "and;" but in the expression *aionas ton aionon*, there is no conjunction. The word *ton*, "of the," is the genitive plural article, and should not be translated "and," as is done in the KJV's "forever and ever." The LXX, at Psa. 90:1, states, *en genea kai genea*, "in generation and generation." Another example of the use of the conjunction *kai*, "and," between the two words for "generation" in the singular. At Heb. 1:8 the noun *aion*, "eon," is used twice in the singular form, but with no "and" between. At Ex. 15:18, *kurios basileuon ton aiona kai ep aiona kai eti*, "the Lord is reigning the eon and upon eon and longer." Eon, as used here, cannot refer to time without end, for there could be nothing beyond, or longer than, endless time. Here the Latin Vulgate says, *Dominus regnabit in aeturnum et ultra*, "The Lord will reign unto [or into] eternity and beyond." The Latin word *in*, when used with an accusative *aeturnum*, has the meaning of placing His reign in eternity, but the *ultra*, "beyond," shows it did not stop when it was placed there, but continued beyond the time of the placing. The English words, "forever and ever," unfortunately, do not convey the same meaning.
The Hebrew text shows, "to the eon and further." Similar expressions appear frequently in the Hebrew, Greek, and Latin texts (see Daniel 12:3, for example).

Wycliffe's version, the first translation into English, did not use the words "forever and ever." Several versions in modern English do not use those words either: ***The Emphasized Bible***, by J.B. Rotherham; ***The N. T., A Translation***, by E.L. Clementson; ***The Emphatic Diaglott***, by Benjamin Wilson; ***Young's Literal Translation***, by Professor Robert Young; and ***The Concordant Literal New Testament***, by A.E. Knoch as well as others.

Chapter Six

What Saith The Translations?

"Because 'orthodox' scholars contradict themselves even within their own organizations, when it comes to these words, it often becomes difficult for sincere students to get their true original meaning."

The Old Scofield Bible, using the KJV, made 35 marginal notations for the noun *aion*, "eon," and three for the adjective *aionios*, "eonian."

The late Oxford University Press ***Sunday School Teacher's Bible*** corrected the noun eighteen times, and the adjective not at all. In the ***Companion Bible***, Dr. E.W. Bullinger noted every occurrence of the noun and the adjective, and showed the corrected translation either in the marginal notes or in the appendix.

In the ***New Analytical Indexed Bible***, by John A. Dickson, there are but three marginal corrections for the noun (1 Cor. 10:11; Heb. 6:5; 9:26). For the adjective only two marginal corrections are given, where "before times eternal" is offered, instead of "before the world began," as in the KJV.

The ***Newberry Bible*** gives many excellent marginal notes. Correct marginal readings appear for the noun, *aion*, more than 100 times. The adjective is left with no marginal notes, except at 1 Tim. 1:9 and Tit. 1:2, where "eternal times" is given.

In Rotherham's 1872 version, the word "age" is used consistently for the noun. In his later edition, 1897, the word "age" is used about 90 times. The adjective for *aion* is translated "age-abiding" quite consistently in both editions.

The ASV of 1901 translates the noun correctly in the text or in a marginal reading in 90 of its 123 occurrences. The adjective was translated "eternal" at Rom. 16:25; 2 Tim. 1:9; and Tit. 1:2, where the KJV used "world."

Professor Robert Young, author of ***Young's Analytical Concordance***, as well as his ***Literal Translation of the Bible***, uses "age" as the translation for the noun. The adjective is translated "age-during" in all except three of its occurrences. At 2 Tim. 1:9 and Tit. 1:2 he uses "time of the ages" and in Philemon, "age-duringly."

J.N. Darby's translation of the New Testament uses "age" 65 times for the noun, but in several instances a correct translation in the text is contradicted in his footnotes.
The ***Concordant Literal Translation of the New Testament*** uses "eon" for the noun consistently, and "eonian" for the adjective in all cases.

The preface of the ***Numeric English New Testament***, by Ivan Panin has this comment (p. 16): "*Aionios* can safely be rendered eternal, but its noun in *eis ton aiona* cannot be rendered 'into eternity' or 'forever;' hence the *aion* phrases are rendered literally." Panin follows his rule, except at Acts 3:21 where he translates the phrase *ap aionos* "from of old," and in John's Evangel, where in eleven occurrences out of thirteen he does exactly what he had said could not be done. The adjective is translated "eternal," except at Rom. 16:25; 2 Tim. 1:9; Tit. 1:2; and Philemon 15.

In the ***New Testament or Covenant***, by E.E. Cunnington, the noun is translated correctly either in the text or in the footnotes twenty-eight times, but "forever" in Matt. 21:19, where it is followed by his note, "Lit. For the age and elsewhere." "For evermore" in this version at Rev. 1:6 is followed by this note: "Lit. to the ages of the ages (and elsewhere)." The first occurrence of the adjective eonian, at Matt. 18:8 he translated "eternal," but this is followed by his note: "Lit. age-long (aeonian) and elsewhere." Thus in Cunnington's version, if the notes are overlooked, one will not see the truth expressed by the Greek text.

Following, are some of the more modern English versions' renderings of these words. For reference purposes, we have listed all the different rendering of the words we are studying. The reader may skip this section if they desire. The manuscript for this book was prepared before several of Bibles which appeared in the 1980's and 1990's came out. That is why they are not included included in this section.

- ***The New International Version*** of the New Testament translates *aion*, "eon," as the following: "forever" 27 times; "age" (including the plural "ages") 25 times; "forever and ever" 22 times; "never" 9 times; "world" 6 times; "eternal" twice, "the universe" twice, "ever" twice; "life" twice; "long ago" twice; and once each with "enduring," "forevermore," and "time began." The adjective is translated "eternal" 60 times; "everlasting" 4 times; "beginning of" twice, as well as once each with "ages past," "forever," life," and "good." This version translates Eph. 3:11, "according to His eternal purpose which He accomplished in Christ Jesus our Lord." Can one explain how God could have an "eternal purpose which He accomplished?" An "eternal purpose" can never be accomplished, and if a purpose has been accomplished it cannot be "eternal."
- In ***The Holy Bible, an American Translation***, by William E. Beck, *aion*, "eon," is translated "forever" 50 times; "world" 29 times; "never" 8 times; "long ago" 3 times; "ever" 4 times; "ages" 4 times; and once each "time," "beginning," and "everlasting." At 1 Cor. 2:6, the noun was not translated, or the translation was so vague one could not tell what word might have been used, although it appears twice in this verse in the text. The adjective is translated "everlasting" 58 times; "forever" 6 times; and once each "long ago," "lasting forever," "world began," "eternally," and "ages ago."

- In ***The Jerusalem Bible***, *aion*, "eon," is translated "forever and ever" 23 times; "forever" 21 times; "world" 19 times; "never" 9 times; "age" 4 times; "time" 3 times; "assured" twice; and once each "eternal," "ever," "ancient times," "world began," "long age," "today," "age began," "last age," "all eternity," "centuries," "world's," "life," and "everything there is." For the adjective there are these: "eternal" 60 times; "everlasting" twice; "eternity" twice; and once each "eternally," "long ago," "endless ages," "beginning of time," and "forever."
- In ***The New American Bible, The New Testament***, by the St. Anthony Guild, 1971 edition, *aion*, "eon," is translated "forever" 24 times; "age" (including the plural "ages") 23 times; "forever and ever" 15 times; "never" 10 times; "world" 9 times; "worldly" 3 times; "endless ages" twice; and once each "enduring," "worldly way," "life demand," "ancient times," "ever," "always," "long ago," "of old," "world's goods," "age-old," "eternity," "without end," "the universe," and "unending ages." The adjective is translated "eternal" 44 times; "everlasting" 17 times; and once each "endless," "without end," " last forever," "endless ages," "ages," "lasting," "lasts forever," and "world began."
- In ***The Good News Bible***, *aion*, "eon," is translated "forever" 23 times; "forever and ever" 22 times; "age" 13 times; "never" 7 times; "long ago" 3 times; "life" 3 times; "eternal" 3 times; "the universe" twice; and once each "now or ever," "live," "all time," "ages of time," "world's," "ever," and "time." The adjective is translated "eternal" 63 times; "beginning of time" twice; and once each "long ages," "lasts forever," " last forever," " all time," and "unfailing."

- In ***The Kingdom Interlinear Translation of the Greek Scriptures***, the noun "eon" is translated "system of things" 33 times; "forever" 28 times; "forever and ever" 20 times; "never" 6 times; "of old" 3 times; "eternity" twice, and once each "of old time," "eternal," "ever," and "indefinite past." The interlinear was translated consistently "age" for the singular and "ages" for the plural. The adjective "eonian" is translated "everlastingly" 65 times; "longlasting" 3 times; and "forever" once. In the interlinear, it is incorrectly translated "everlasting," except at Philemon 15 where it is "everlasting(ly)."

This is a time of apostasy, so while some groups do teach and believe the truth concerning the eons, others have departed from what the Scriptures say, not only about the eons, but also about equally vital truths.

Although it would seem several translators, such as those cited above, realize that *aion* and *aionios* cannot be construed to mean endless time, yet they refuse to use a word which more closely expresses the Greek. Rather, they have chosen to use the inconsistent renderings that have been shown in this book. The learned Catholic men who translated and authorized ***The Jerusalem Bible*** and ***The New American Bible*** seem to be oblivious of the fact that the large Catholic Bible dictionary titled, ***The Encyclopedic Dictionary of the Bible*** says (p. 693):

ETERNITY: The Bible hardly speaks of eternity in the philosophical sense of infinite duration without beginning or end. The Hebrew word olam, which is used alone (Ps. 61:8; etc.) or with various prepositions (Gen. 3:22; etc.) in contexts where it is traditionally translated as 'forever,' means in itself no more than 'for an indefinitely long period.' Thus me olam does not mean 'from eternity' but 'of old' (Gen. 6:4, etc.). In the N.T. aion is used as the equivalent of olam.

Here the translators have consistently ignored what their own "authorities" tells them, and have used words which *do* convey the idea of endless time. Because "orthodox" scholars contradict themselves even within their own organizations, when it comes to these words, it often becomes difficult for sincere students to get their true original meaning. The following letter illustrates the point.

Chapter Seven

Eonian Means What? A Search For Truth

"By this point in my studying I had begun to think that possibly these theologians were employing more subterfuge than enlightened honesty in dealing with the issue."

Dear Louis,

Greetings in the name of our Lord Jesus Christ! I read that you are to be a speaker at the upcoming Bible conference close to Springfield, MO. I'm writing to say that I now plan on attending on Saturday, if possible. I look forward to meeting you.

I enjoyed our correspondence of three years ago and have not forgotten the nature or substance of your thoughts expressed then. Here is the result of my thinking and studying on aionios in recent times. For some years (I'm 32 yrs. old) certain passages had made me wonder as to the scope of their meaning; i.e. Romans 5, 1 Cor 15, Colossians 1, etc. In 1976 I received some sample literature, among which were tracts on the Salvation of All. Being a "Bible believing" orthodox evangelical, I rejected the idea. The year 1979 found me just having completed a year of studying the Koine (Greek) language at a theological seminary. Thus new tools were provided to eventually consider the idea of God being All in all.

As I began to seriously ponder this concept (which I felt no particular desire to adopt), I began to read more literature, books, pamphlets by others that were well reasoned from Scripture. I began to be convinced in spite of my previous feelings. I decided I had better read the "pro-eternal torment" position.

What do scholars of this position present? Clouded and confused thoughts. First I read a classic by William G.T. Shedd entitled ***The Doctrine of Endless Punishment****. This was supposed by evangelicals to be the best defense of the foregoing doctrine. His first section in which he appealed to the "Church Fathers" I soon discounted, for as anyone who is even marginally aware of "the Fathers" can testify: they proclaim many diverse and even esoteric doctrines. The book did help me realize that one of the keys to resolving the question was the meaning of the word aionios. Does it mean eternal (endless) or eonian (age-lasting)? This is very critical. After much discussion, Shedd's conclusion as per page 84:* anything, *endless* or *limited, can be denominated aionios! Both ways! It depends on the passage. And, of course, only a competent exegete such as Shedd can determine which of the two opposite meanings is to be chosen in a particular passage. There was no help for me here. What other conclusions did he come to? Page 145, "'If there were no God, we should be compelled to invent one' is now a familiar sentiment. 'If there were no hell, we should be compelled to invent one' is equally true." What else does this scholar say? Page 159, "the Bible teaches that there will always be some sin, and some death, in the universe." It's as if he had never read 1 Corinthians*

15:26. One final quote from Shedd, Page 119: "Nothing is requisite for (doctrine of endless torments) maintenance but the admission of three cardinal truths of theism; namely, that there is a just God; that man has free will; and that sin is a voluntary action." He did not give a Scriptural reverence of Romans 11:32 for this statement. In fact, he gave no reference to the Scriptures at this point.

I thought I might read a more recent book of Endless Punishment--so I read a highly recommended ***Doctrine of Eternal Punishment*** *to gather more information on aionios. Page 49, "No sound Greek scholar can pretend that aionios means anything less than eternal." I decided he must not have read Shedd's book. Also the very highly esteemed translators of the New International Version must not have read the latter book (or must not be "sound Greek scholars") because their rendering in Romans 16:25 speaks about, "the mystery hidden from long ages past." "Long Ages Past" being their translation "eonian times." I was confused--one meaning only (eternal) or two (opposite) meanings? Well, in our Greek class we learned to trust the Arndt-Gingrich Lexicon to settle the questions that came to mind. I was curious--would Arndt-Gingrich say* one *or* two *meanings? The answer:* three *meanings: 1) endless past with definite ending point in the future, 2) definite beginning point in past with endless future, 3) endless past and endless future! Ingenious! By this point in my studying I had begun to think that possibly these theologians were employing more subterfuge than enlightened honesty in dealing with the issue. Most other reference works fall into one of the afore-mentioned categories when dealing with aionios. Of course, there are the King James Version's "world began" phrases.*

I cannot yet give you a conclusion to this whole matter from a personal perspective, but I think it will be obvious to you which direction my thinking is headed. In search of truth,

Mike

Chapter Eight

Greek Tools

"...concerning zeal, persecuting the church; concerning the righteousness which is the law, blameless. But what things were gain to me, these I have counted loss for Christ. Yet indeed I also count all things loss for the excellence of the knowledge of Christ Jesus my Lord, for whom I suffered the loss of all things, and count them as rubbish, that I may gain Christ and be found in Him, not having my own righteousness, which is from the law, but that which is through faith in Christ, the righteousness which is from God through faith; that I may know Him and the power of His resurrection, and the fellowship of His sufferings, being conformed to His death, if by any means, I may attain to the resurrection from the dead.
-Philippians 3:7-11

The man who wrote the words above was Paul, the apostle. Paul, was a theologian. He studied under one of the all-time greats in his day. Gamaliel, Paul's professor, so to speak, knew the Scriptures in their original language. He was the head of what today we would call a seminary. Gamaliel was an outstanding scholar. Yet Gamaliel could not bring Paul to the truth. Paul counted his Hebrew studies as rubbish.

Now Paul did not throw all his training away. But apart from the spirit of revelation, the Scriptures did not reveal the truth. Paul tells us that God is love. Paul did not know such a God under Gamaliel.

Once Paul received that love, he was able to use that which he learned from scholars to the good of those who Paul would teach. The Book of Romans is a perfect example of the right balance between revelation and scholarship.

I urge those of you who are reading this book to learn the difference between revelation and scholarship. The church world is full of Gamaliels, Hillels, and Shammais (great ancient Hebrew scholars). They write many books which are but rubbish apart from the spirit of revelation.

So then, a word to the wise. Set your priorities. Knowing Christ will not come from scholarship; it will come from relationship. Once the intimate relationship is established, language tools can become very valuable to instruct the hungry.

While not everyone has the time to study Hebrew and Greek, which require years of study before one can become proficient in either language, there are excellent study aids available to the English reader with which one can check to see how each Greek or Hebrew word has been translated in its every occurrence in the Scripture. Christian book stores, or book stores for the denominational groups, have such study aids as these:

The Word Study N.T., in two volumes. Volume one shows the translation of each word used in the KJV in large print with a code number under each English word. That number is keyed to volume two and to several other Greek lexicons and concordances. Volume two is titled ***The Word Study Concordance***. It is a copy of the old ***Englishman's Greek Concordance of the New Testament***.

Also available are Strong's ***Exhaustive Concordance***; Young's ***Analytical Concordance***; ***The Englishman's Greek Concordance of the New Testament; The Englishman's Hebrew and Chaldee Concordance of the Old Testament*** and Smith's ***Greek-English Concordance***. These works contain a complete listing of each New Testament Greek word, or each Old Testament Hebrew word, so that one may see at a glance how the words were translated in the KJV.

The Concordant Literal New Testament with Keyword Concordance lists each word of the Greek text and shows how it was translated in that version.

Word Study volumes, of which there are many are also very helpful. ***Vincent's Word Studies of the New Testament*** is one that I would highly recommend.

Careful study of some of the volumes previously mentioned will glean facts often overlooked or purposely avoided in traditional "Bible Study." For example, the Young's ***Analytical Concordance*** plainly reveals what I have been saying about the words we are looking at. A search under "eternal" will reveal that Dr. Young clearly saw that the King's translators did not handle the word aion correctly. A look in ***Smith's Greek-English Concordance*** under entry number 165b will reveal much which the average person who reads the King James Bible will never become aware of.

While interlinear Bibles are not the complete answer, they often help to at least look at the Greek and Hebrew underlying the translations. ***The Greek New Testament (UBS4 with NRSV & NIV)*** edited by John Kohlenberger III, ***The Greek-English Interlinear New Testament*** edited by J.D. Douglas which contains the United Bible Society's fourth edition of their Greek text along side the NRSV, and the ***Zondervan Parallel New Testament in Greek and English*** which contains the Nestle's Greek text, a literal translation, the KJV, and the NIV, are helpful with the New Testament. ***The Interlinear NIV Hebrew-English Old Testament*** is helpful in the Old Testament.

Throughout this book, I have quoted many dozens of scholars adept in the languages of the Bible. It would behoove the readers to acquaint themselves with some of these very valuable resources.

Chapter Nine

Aion in Greek Literature

"If by 'eonian,' endless time were meant, then what could be more than endless time?"

"All the way through it is never feasible to understand 'aionios' as everlasting."
-Dr. Nigel Turner

"In Hebrew and Greek, the words rendered 'everlasting' have not this sense. They signify a long duration of time, a period; whence the phrase, during these eternities and beyond."
-Dr. Lammenois

Ancient writings, other than the Scriptures, show how *aion* and *aionios* were used in the ordinary affairs of that time period. Long ago in Rome, periodic games were held. These were referred to as "secular" games. Herodian, who wrote in Greek about the end of the second century A.D., called these *aionios*, "eonian," games. In no sense could those games have been eternal.

Adolph Deissman gives this account: "Upon a lead tablet found in the Necropolis at Adrumetum in the Roman province of Africa, near Carthage, the following inscription, belonging to the early third century, is scratched in Greek: 'I am adjuring Thee, the great God, the eonian, and more than eonian (*epaionion*) and almighty...' If by eonian, endless time were meant, then what could be more than endless time?"

In the ***Apostolical Constitutions***, a work of the fourth century A.D., it is said, *kai touto humin esto nomimon aionion hos tes suntleias to aionos*, "And let this be to you an eonian ordinance until the consummation of the eon." Obviously there was no thought in the author's mind of endless time.

Dr. Agar Beet, in his article "On the Future Punishment of Sin," published in ***The Expositor***, carefully examined the meaning of the word *aionios*, and the only passage in which Dr. Beet could adduce the word could *possibly* mean endless was from Plato's Laws (p. 904 A). But there is a question there as to whether Plato was referring to endless time.

The noun and adjective we are studying were used repeatedly in the Septuagint in relation to ordinances and laws which were limited as to time. A check of these usages as given in a concordance to the Septuagint will show there is no instance in which these words can refer to endlessness.

There are those who insist that the "punishments" of God are "forever and ever." The Greek word for punish and punishment appears just three times in the N.T. Each time, the punishing comes at the hands of humans, not from God. There is no word meaning "punish" or "punishment" in the Hebrew. However, our common version translates two Greek words, *timoreo*, "punish," and *kalazo*, "chastise," with the same English word, "punish." Chastising carries the idea of correcting with a view to amendment of one's mistakes, while punishment is penal action. These two words were defined by Aristotle in his Rhet. 1, 10, 17, as, "*kolasis* is corrective, *timoria* alone is the satisfaction of the inflictor." Archbishop Trench states in his synonyms of the N.T. (p. 23-24): "*timorio* indicates the vindictive character of punishment; *kolasis* indicates punishment as it has reference to correcting and bettering the offender." *Kolasin* is the word our Lord used as recorded at Matt. 25:46 which the King James tradition mistranslates "everlasting punishment". *Timoreo* is used at Acts 22:5; 26:11; and *timoria* at Heb. 10:29.

In Ex. 15:18, where the KJV says: "The Lord shall reign forever and ever," the Septuagint shows, *kurios basileuon ton aiona kai ap aiona kai eti*, "The Lord is reigning the eon, and upon eon, and longer," and the Latin Vulgate, *in aeternum et ultra*, "into eternity and beyond." The Hebrew says, "Jehovah shall reign to the eon and beyond." Our conception of the English "forever and ever" allows for no time to be "beyond."

Some insist that while the noun in the singular does mean "age," in the plural it means "forever," or "eternal." But notice how both the singular and the plural are used in the Septuagint. At Micah 4:5 (singular), *eis ton aiona kai epekeina*, "for the eon and beyond," and at Dan. 12:3 (plural), *eis tous aionas kai eti*, "for the eons and longer." If the plural means forever, eternity, endless time etc., there can be no time longer than that. In the Book of Enoch there is, *heos suntelesthê krima tou aionos ton aionon*, "until the judgment of the eon of the eons may be accomplished." The Greek word *suntelesthê* is a compound word (*sun* + *telesthê*). Without the *sun*, *telestha* appears at Luke 12:50; Rev. 10:7; 17:17; 20:3,5, and 7 where it should be translated: "should be accomplished" (or "finished" or "consummated"). The *heos* of the above is a conjunction of time, which limits the judgment to a period called "the eon of the eons." Paul uses both the singular and the plural form in one sentence (Eph. 3:21), "to Him be glory in the ecclesia and in Christ Jesus for all the generations of the eon of the eons" (CV). Understand that as long as there are "generations," we are not at the end of all things and therefore "eon of the eons" cannot refer to eternity, everlasting, forever and ever, etc.

At Isa. 60:15, the adjective is used: "I will make you an eonian (*aionion*) excellency." This is followed by, "a joy of many generations." Eonian cannot mean endlessness here, for when the eons close, generations cease for there will be no more procreation. Dr. Mangey, a translator of the writings of Philo, says Philo did not use *aionios* to express endless duration.

Josephus shows that *aionios* did not mean endlessness, for he uses it of the period between the giving of the law to Moses and that of his own writing; to the period of the imprisonment of the tyrant John by the Romans; and to the period during which Herod's temple stood. The temple had already been destroyed by the time Josephus was writing.

St. Gregory of Nyssa speaks of *aionios diastêma*, "an eonian interval." It would be absurd to call an interval "endless."

St. Chrysostum, in his homily on Eph. 2:1-3, says that "Satan's kingdom is æonian; that is, it will cease with the present world."

St. Justin Martyr repeatedly used the word *aionios* as in the Apol. (p. 57), *aionion kolasin ...all ouchi chiliontaetê periodon*, "eonian chastening ...but a period, not a thousand years." Or, as some translate the last clause: "but a period of a thousand years only." He limits the eonian chastening to a period of a thousand years, rather than to endlessness.

In 1 Enoch 10:10 there is an interesting statement using the Greek words: *zoên aionion*, "life eonian," or, as in the KJV, "everlasting life" (at John 3:16 and elsewhere). The whole sentence in Enoch is, *hoti elpizousi zêsai zoên aionion, kai hoti zêsetai hekastos auton etê pentakosia*, "For they hope to live an eonian life, and that each one of them will live five hundred years." Here, eonian life is limited to five hundred years! In the N.T. eonian life is limited to life during the eons, after which death will be destroyed by making ALL alive IN CHRIST, incorruptible and immortal.

Chapter Ten

Bibles Without "Everlasting Punishment"

"And these shall go away into punishment of the ages, but the righteous into life of the ages."
-New Testament in Modern Speech

"And these shall be coming away into chastening eonian, yet the just into life eonian."
-Concordant Literal Translation

"And these shall go away to punishment age-during, but the righteous to life age-during."
-Young's Literal Translation

It is sad to note, but nevertheless true, that most Christians do not realize there are very dramatic differences in translation from one Bible to another. We have heard so often that the "inspired" or "inerrant" Word of God is basically the same in all translations. This is just not true. But one will not see this unless they place several side by side and make some comparisons. Listed below are a few translations which we will compare to the King James Bible on the verse Matthew 26:46.

- Concerning the duration of chastening, Matt. 25:46 says (KJV), *"And these shall go away into everlasting punishment, but the righteous into life eternal."*

- Scarlett's ***New Testament*** written in 1792 has "aeonian punishment" in place to "everlasting punishment." *"And these will go away into aeonian punishment: but the righteous into aeonian life."*

- The ***New Covenant*** by Dr. J.W. Hanson written in 1884 renders Matt. 25:46: *"And these shall go away into aeonian chastisement, and the just into aeonian life."*

- Young's ***Literal Translation*** first published in 1898 and reprinted many times since uses the following words: *"And these shall go away to punishment age-during, but the righteous to life age-during."* Professor Young also compiled ***Young's Concordance***, wherewith one can check the translation of each Hebrew or Greek word as translated in the KJV.

- The ***Twentieth Century New Testament*** first printed in the year 1900 has: *"And these last will go away 'into aeonian punishment,' but the righteous 'into aeonian life.'"*

- ***The Holy Bible in Modern English*** by Ferrar Fenton first published in 1903 gives the rendering: *"And these He will dismiss into a long correction, but the well-doers to an enduring life.*

- ***The New Testament in Modern Speech***, by Dr. Weymouth, says: *"And these shall go away into punishment of the ages, but the righteous into life of the ages."*

Dr. Weymouth most frequently adopts such terms as "life of the ages," "fire of the ages;" and in Rev. 14:6, "The good news of the ages." It is a matter to regret that the editors of the most recent edition of Dr. Weymouth's version have reverted to the KJV renderings for the passages containing the Greek word *aion*, eon, or age.

- ***The Western New Testament*** published in 1926 renders Matt. 25:46 as follows: *"And these will go away into eternal punishment, but the righteous into life eternal."*

The translation, however, has a footnote on Matthew 21:19 on the word "forever" which is the same word for "eternal" which says: *"Literally, for the age (and elsewhere).* This Bible does not use the word "Hell" at all.

- Clementson's ***The New Testament*** (1938) shows, *"And these shall go away into eonian correction, but the righteous into eonian life."*

- Wilson's ***Emphatic Diaglott*** (1942 edition) translates the verse, *"And these shall go forth to the aionian cutting-off; but the righteous to aionian life."*

It should be noted that the "cutting-off" refers to pruning a fruit tree to make it bear more fruit. The idea behind the word is not destructive but *productive*! Had Jesus wanted to emphasize a destructive end, He would have used the word *timoria.*

- ***The Concordant Version*** (1930): *"And these shall be coming away into chastening eonian, yet the just into life eonian."*

- ***The New Testament of our Lord and Savior Jesus Anointed*** printed in 1958 says: *"And these shall go away into age-lasting cutting-off and the just into age-lasting life."*

- Rotherham, in his ***Emphasized Bible*** (1959), translates this verse, *"and these shall go away into age-abiding correction, but the righteous into age-abiding life."*

- ***The Restoration of Original Sacred Name Bible*** copyrighted in 1976 has "age-abiding correction" instead of the incorrect and quite frankly, blasphemous "everlasting punishment." This phrase "everlasting punishment," when one really thinks about it, renders the work of Christ worthless. It says that His forgiveness, His love, His grace, His mercy, the power of His blood, all these and more become limited when one translates "aionion kolasin" as "everlasting punishment." *"And these shall go away -abiding correction, but the righteous into age-abiding life."*

There are other Bible translations besides these which have either completely eliminated the concept of eternal punishment from their pages, or have made great strides towards wiping this pagan concept off God's Word. Even some King James Study Bibles will show the reader in the margins or appendixes that the King's translators were incorrect in their rendering of "eternal punishment" and "Hell." The great *Companion Bible* by Dr. Bullinger is an example of that.

In summary, then, as we gain more knowledge of the Greek and Hebrew languages, the pagan concept of "eternal punishment" is becoming manifest as a pagan concept which cannot be found in the original languages of the Bible. Therefore, more and more of the translations printed since the King James Bible of 1611 have dramatically departed from the King's translators translations for words closer to the actual Greek and Hebrew meanings rather than "tradition." The word "Hell," for example, has almost completely disappeared from most translations in the Old Testament. It occurs in most translations only 11 to 14 times and not at all in many translations. The day will come when the pagan concept of "Hell" will no longer be found in any Bible translation. It wasn't in the original languages. The foundation of the Bible, that is, the Old Testament, knows of no such place. Why should we perpetuate Greek, Roman, Egyptian, Babylonian, and Anglo-Saxon mythology? This is where the concept came from. Here is where the word "Hell," the goddess of the underworld, came from. Leave it there. This idea does not belong on the previous pages of our Bibles.

Chapter Eleven

Verses "Proving" Punishment Will be Everlasting

"Professor A.T. Robertson and A.B. Bruce agree that 'kolasis aionion' of the KJV has a literal meaning of 'age-lasting correction.'"

"Let me say to Bible students that we must be very careful how we use the word 'eternity.' We have fallen into great error in our constant usage of that word. There is no word in the whole Book of God corresponding with our eternal..."
-G. Campbell Morgan

Matthew 25:31-46 concerns the judgment of NATIONS, not individuals. It is to be distinguished from other judgments mentioned in Scripture, such as the judgment of the saints (2 Cor. 5:10-11); the second resurrection, and the great white throne judgment (Rev. 20:11-15). The judgment of the nations is based upon their treatment of the Lord's brethren (verse 40). No resurrection of the dead is here, just nations living at the time. To apply verses 41 and 46 to mankind as a whole is an error. Perhaps it should be pointed out at this time that the Fundamentalist Evangelical community at large has made the error of gathering many Scriptures which speak of various judgments which will occur in different ages and assigning them all to "Great White Throne" judgment. This is a serious mistake. Matthew 25:46 speaks nothing of "grace through faith." We will leave it up to the reader to decide who the "Lord's brethren" are, but final judgment based upon the receiving of the Life of Christ is not the subject matter of Matthew 25:46 and should not be interjected here. Even if it were, the penalty is "age-during correction" and not "everlasting punishment."

Dr. J.D. Dummelow, in his commentary on Matt. 25:31-46, says, "Christ here speaks of the judgment of Christians alone, because that was the question which most concerned the apostles and their future converts... A common interpretation, however, is that the judgment of all mankind is meant."

Professor A.T. Robertson, in his **Word Pictures in the N.T.**, and Prof. A.B. Bruce, in **The Expositor's Greek Testament**, agree that the kolasis aionion, the "everlasting punishment" of the KJV, has a literal meaning of "age-lasting correction."

Dr. F.W. Farrar says: "It may be worthwhile, however, to point out once more to less educated readers that aion, aionios, and their Hebrew equivalents in all combinations are repeatedly used of things which have come to an end. Even Augustine admits (what, indeed, no one can deny), that in Scripture aion and aionios must in many instances mean 'having an end,' and St. Gregory of Nyssa, who at least knew Greek, uses aionios as the epithet for 'an interval.'" Dean Farrar also states: "The pages of theologians in all ages show a startling prevalence of such terms as 'everlasting death, everlasting damnation, everlasting torments, everlasting vengeance, everlasting fire' - not one of which has Scriptural authority." Dr. Farrar was well versed in the Biblical languages, author of books on the life of Jesus, the life of Paul, and Greek grammar, as well as others.

Dr. Edwin Abbott, headmaster of the City of London School, wrote in his **Cambridge Sermons** (p. 25), "And as for ourselves, though occasionally mentioning in language general and metaphorical, states of eonian life and eonian chastisement awaiting us after death, the Holy Scriptures give no detailed information as to either condition."
Dr. Abbott's conviction, as expressed, showed he thought the received dogma was untenable. An argument was introduced by Augustine, and since his day incessantly repeated, that if aionios kolasis does not mean "endless punishment," then there is no security for the believer that aionios zoe means "endless life," and that he will enjoy the promise of endless happiness. But Matt. 25:46 shows the "eonian chastisement" and "eonian life" are of the same duration-lasting during the eons, and when the eons end, as Scripture states they will (1 Cor. 10:11; Heb. 9:26), the time called "eonian" is past and the life called "eonian" is finished, but life continues beyond the eons, as Paul teaches at 1 Cor. 15:26: "The last enemy that shall be destroyed is death." That is, the last, the final one in order. How will it be destroyed? First Corinthians 15:22 gives the answer: "For as IN ADAM ALL are dying, even so IN CHRIST ALL shall be made alive." Death is destroyed when ALL have been vivified, or made alive, IN CHRIST. There will then be no more death. Just as life is destroyed by death, so death is destroyed by life. Our present bodies are mortal and corruptible (1 Cor. 15:44-55), but when mankind is made alive IN CHRIST they will be raised immortal and incorruptible.

Those who believe in a universal salvation as is spoken of at Col. 1:15-20, and see the purpose of God's love and His plan for the eons, are secure in their belief that the same number of those who are now dying as a result of Adam's disobedience will be made alive in Christ. The ALL of these verses represent exactly the same number of mankind. Romans 5:18-19 says, "by the offense of one, judgment came upon all men - by the righteousness of One the free gift came upon all men - by one man's disobedience the many were made sinners, so by the obedience of One shall the many be made righteous." The "all men" and the "many" in these verses include the same number of humans in both cases.

The "all" in 1 Cor. 15:22; Col. 1:15-22; and Rom. 5:18-19 mean the same in every case. God's eonian purpose is to head up ALL in the Christ, as is stated in Eph. 1:9-10 and 3:11.

Dr. Alford Plumer's **An Exegetical Commentary on the Gospel of Matthew** (pp. 351-352): "It is often pointed out that 'eternal' (aionios) in 'eternal punishment' must have the same meaning as in 'eternal life.' No doubt, but that does not give us the right to say that 'eternal' in both cases means 'endless.'"

Dr. G. Campbell Morgan, preacher, teacher, evangelist, and author; sometimes called the "prince of expositors," wrote in his **Studies of the Four Gospels** concerning Matt. 25:31-46, "Then, moreover, we must be careful not to read into this section of prophecy things which it does not contain; for while it has been interpreted as though it were a description of the final judgment, the Great White Throne-These shall go away into age-abiding punishment; but the righteous into age-abiding life-the terms are co-equal in value, and whatever one means the other means. Only remember that here Christ is not dealing with the subject of the soul's destiny either in heaven or hell. They are terms that have to do wholly with the setting up of the kingdom here in this world..." In Dr. Morgan's, **God's Methods with Men**, he says (pp. 185-186), "Let me say to Bible students that we must be very careful how we use the word 'eternity.' We have fallen into great error in our constant usage of that word. There is no word in the whole Book of God corresponding with our 'eternal,' which as commonly used among us, means absolutely without end." In his book, **The Corinthian Letters of Paul**, the same author states concerning 1 Cor. 15:22 (p. 191): "The word Adam is used here in the sense of headship of a race, the one from whom the race springs. But God's second Man was the last Adam. If we say second Adam, we presuppose the possibility of a third Adam, another from whom a race shall spring. There will be none such. It is 'first Adam' and 'last Adam.' What does relationship with Him mean? In the program of God all are to be made alive in Christ." Sir Robert Anderson, a writer on eschatology, says, "The N.T. unfolds an economy of times and seasons; many ages head up in the one great age, within which the manifold purpose of God, in relation to earth, shall be fulfilled. Here, these words eon, age are applicable, and are used."

Dr. Edward Plumptre, an eschatologist, wrote, "I fail to find, as is used by the Greek Fathers, any instance in which the idea of time duration is unlimited."

Dr. William White says, "That of the widely different subjects to which aeonian is applied in the N.T., in 70 they are of a limited and temporary nature."
Professor Knappe of Halle wrote, "The Hebrew was destitute of any single word to express endless duration. The pure idea of eternity is not found in any of the ancient languages."

Professor Hermann Oldhausen said, "The Bible has no expression for endlessness. All the Biblical terms imply or denote long periods." Dr. Oldhausen was a German Lutheran theologian.

Lexicographers note the fact that it was not until the fifth century A.D. that theologians began to read the sense of endlessness into Bible words. Dr. Lewis S. Chafer deplores the difficulty that the average reader of the Bible will encounter in seeking to understand the real meaning of these passages, when he notes how hopelessly the KJV has obscured the word aion. He said, "The word, which in common usage has a limited meaning, is used by the translators as the one English rendering for at least four widely differing ideas in the original. So that if the truth contained in this important body of Scripture is to be understood, the student must not only know the various meanings which are expressed by the one word, but also be able to determine the correct use of it in the many passages in which it occurs. Therefore, the KJV has placed the simple truth they contain beyond the average reader of the Bible. The English word 'world,' as used in the New Testament, may mean a distinct period of time, commonly known as an age (as its original is a few times translated), or it may refer to the things created: the earth, its inhabitants, or their institution. The ages are often referred to in Scripture, and the study of the exact conditions and purposes of each of them are not fanciful; but it is rather the only adequate foundation for any true knowledge of the Bible."

Dr. W.H. Griffith Thomas wrote in **The Christian**, in a comment upon Heb. 11:3, "the word rendered 'worlds' is 'ages' and refers not so much to the material creation as to the world regarded from the standpoint of time... The last mentioned (age, aion) is the name used here, and it seems to refer to what may be called time-worlds, the idea being that of various ages or dispensations being planned by God with reference to a goal toward which all are moving."

Dr. Thomas' notes on Rom. 5:18-19 were, "As mankind's connection with Adam involved him in certain death, through sin, so his relation to Christ insures to him life without fail. The double headship of mankind in Adam and Christ show the significance of the work of redemption for the entire race."

Professor Max Muller says in reference to the Latin word aeternum, "that it originally signified life or time, but has given rise to a number of words expressing eternity-the very opposite of life and time." He says the Latin aevum, that is, the Greek word "ainon, later aion, became the name of time, age, and its derivative, aeviternus, or aeternus, was made to express eternity."

Dr. Isaac Watts says, "There is not one place in Scripture which occurs to me, where the word death necessarily signifies a certain miserable immortality of the soul."

Professor Taylor Lewis states, "The conception of absolute endlessness as etymological of *olam* or eon would clearly have prevented plurals." He continues, "'ever' (German: ewig), was originally a noun denoting age, just like the Greek, Latin and Hebrew words corresponding to it." Dr. Lewis wrote an interesting article for **Lange's Commentary** about the use of the words olam and aion as used at Ecc. 1:4.

Jeremy Taylor, a hell-fire advocate wavers, and after his ebullient flashes of **Systematic Hellology**, is constrained to the following modification in **Jeremy Taylor's Works** (vol. 3, p. 43), "Though the fire is everlasting, not all that enters it is everlasting," then adds, "The word everlasting signifies only to the end of its period." Would that other hell-fire advocates were so honest.

Chapter Twelve

Scholars Acknowledge Restitution of All

"(ta panta) all men: The phrase must not be limited in any way. It cannot mean merely 'Gentiles as well as Jews,' or 'the elect,' or 'all who believe.' We must receive it as it stands."
-Dr. Brooke Foss Westcott

"Under the instruction of those great teachers many other theologians believed in universal salvation; and indeed the whole Eastern Church until after 500 A.D. was inclined to it."

- Dr. Brooke Foss Westcott says of John 12:32, in the ***Speaker's Commentary***: "(*ta panta*) all men: The phrase must not be limited in any way. It cannot mean merely 'Gentiles as well as Jews,' or 'the elect,' or 'all who believe.' We must receive it as it stands (Rom. 5:18; 8:32; 2 Cor. 5:15; Eph. 1:10; 1 Tim. 2:6; Heb. 2:9; 1 John 2:2). The remarkable reading 'all things' (*omnia*) points to a still wider application of Redemption (Col. 1:20)."

- John MacIntyre, in his book ***Christian Doctrine of History***, wrote (pp. 5-6), "What we regard as the Biblical view of time and history can only by anachronism be said to be that of the biblical writers themselves, yet that is the anachronism of which so many of our contemporaries are guilty."

- G.T. Stevenson, in his ***Time and Eternity***, says (p. 63), "Since, as we have seen, the noun *aion* refers to a period of time, it appears very improbable that the derived adjective *aionios* would indicate infinite duration, nor have we found any evidence in Greek writing to show that such a concept was expressed by this term." And on page 72, "In 1 Cor. 15:22-29 the inspired apostle to the Gentiles transports his readers' thoughts far into the future, beyond the furthest point envisaged elsewhere in holy writ. After outlining the triumph of the Son of God in bringing all creation under His benign control, Paul sets forth the consummation of the divine plan of the ages in four simple, yet infinitely profound words, 'God all in all.' This is our God, purposeful, wise, loving and almighty, His Son our Lord a triumphant Savior, Who destroys His enemies by making them friends."

- Professor William Barclay comments in his ***The Letter to the Corinthians***, concerning 1 Cor. 15:22-28, "God sent forth His Son to redeem the world so in the end God will receive back a world redeemed and then there will be nothing in heaven or in earth outside the love and power of God."

- From ***The New Schaff-Herzog Encyclopedia of Religious Knowledge*** comes (vol. 12, p. 96), "Under the instruction of those great teachers many other theologians believed in universal salvation; and indeed the whole Eastern Church until after 500 A.D. was inclined to it. Doederlein says that 'In proportion as any man was eminent in learning in Christian antiquity, the more did he cherish and defend the hope of the termination of future torments.'" Many more church historians could be quoted with similar observations.

- Concise summaries of universal salvation appear in the ***Schaff-Herzog Encyclopedia***, vol. 12, pp. 95-97; and in the McClintock and Strong ***Encyclopedia of Biblical, Theological, and Ecclesiastical Literature***, vol. 10, pp. 656-665.

- Karl Barth, in his book ***Christ and Adam, Man and Humanity***, wrote concerning Romans 5 (p. 109), "But in vv. 12-21 Paul does not limit his context to Christ's relationship to believers, but gives fundamentally the same account of His relationship to all men. The context is widened from church history to world history, from Christ's relationship to Christians to all men. ...What is said here applies generally and universally, and not merely to one limited group of men. Here 'religious' presuppositions are not once hinted at. The fact of Christ is here presented as something that dominates and includes all men." On page 112 of the same work: "vv. 12-21 are revolutionary in their insistence that what is true of Christians must also be true of all men."

- Professor Marvin Vincent, in his ***Word Studies in the N.T.***, commenting upon Col. 1:20 wrote (vol. 3, p. 471), "All things (*ta panta*) must be taken in the same sense as in vv. 16, 17, 18. The whole universe, material and spiritual. The range of discussion opened by these words is too wide to be entered upon here. Paul's declarations elsewhere as to the ultimate fate of evil men and angels, must certainly be allowed their full weight; yet such passages as this and Eph. 1:10 seem to point to a larger purpose of God in redemption than is commonly conceived." And in vol. 4, p. 291, about 2 Tim. 1:9: "Before the world began (*pro chronon aionion*) Lit. Before eternal times. If it is insisted that *aionion* means everlasting, this statement is absurd. It is impossible that anything should take place before everlasting times." In vol. 4, pp. 58-62, commenting upon the Greek word *aion*, he says, "*Aion*, transliterated aion, is a period of time, of longer or shorter duration, having a beginning and an end, and complete in itself.... The word always carries the notion of time and not eternity. It always means a period of time. The adjective *aionios* in like manner carries the idea of time. Neither the noun nor the adjective, in themselves, carries the sense of endless or everlasting... *aionios* means enduring through, or pertaining to, a period of time. Both the noun and the adjective are applied to limited periods."

- Dr. S.S. Graig, in ***The Presbyterian***, Jan. 30, 1930, wrote, "According to the latter (Dr. B.B. Warfield), there is no warrant for saying that the Scriptures teach that but few are saved, and that while some will be lost, yet that when the Scriptures say that Christ came to save the world, that He does save the world and that the world shall be saved by Him. They mean that He came to save and does save the human race, and that the human race is being led by God to a racial salvation, that in the age-long development of the race of men, it will attain at last to a complete salvation, and our eyes will be greeted with the spectacle of a saved world. Thus the human race attains to the goal for which it was created, and sin does not snatch it out of God's hands; the primal purpose of God with it is fulfilled; and through Christ the race of men, though fallen into sin, is recovered to God, and fulfills its original destiny."

- Dr. Warfield believed what Paul taught in 1 Tim. 4:9-11: "This is a faithful saying and worthy of all acceptation. For therefore we both labor and suffer reproach, because we trust in the living God, Who is the Savior of ALL men. Specially of those that believe. These things command and teach." While Dr. Warfield spent most of his life teaching the Calvinist "election doctrine" which usually meant few would be saved, it seems Dr. Warfield softened up quite a bit in his latter years.

This is a phenomenon which seems to occur quite frequently with dogmatic minds. Time and wisdom have a way of tempering the zealot's demand for justice. As the zealot wanders through his own sins and lifelong character flaws which he seems never to be able to overcome, he looks for mercy for himself, and in so doing, discovers that same fountain of mercy flows to all mankind. God becomes bigger as we become smaller.

- Dr. J.R. Dummelow, in his commentary of Col. 1:20: "The Son's atoning death, availed for the whole angelic world, as well as for the world of men, since the Son is head of both. Very difficult." Although the Dr. admits the truth of universal reconciliation, it is "very difficult" for him to do so from his denominational position.

- St. Clemens of Alexandria says, "He saves all, but converting some by punishment, and others who follow by their own will-that every knee may bend to Him, of things in heaven and earth and under the earth." (See Phil. 2:9-12)

- St. Isadore states, "When the Lord says 'neither in this world nor in the world to come' He shows that, for some, sins are there to be forgiven." (Read Matt. 12:31-32)

- John Scotus Erigena said, "This, however we say, not that nature will be happy in all, but that in all it will be set free from death and misery."

- St. Anselm: "It is not just that God should altogether suffer to perish His creatures which He has made. God demands from no sinner more than he owes; but since no one can pay as much as he owes, Christ alone paid for all more than the debt due."

- Professor Friedrich D.F. Schleiermacher says, "Through the force of the Redemption, a universal restoration of souls will follow."

- Perrone stated, "All agree in saying that it is too violent to admit at once into heaven all those who only repented of their past evil life at the end, and who indulged too much in the sensualities of this life, since nothing defiled enters there; also it is too harsh to assign all such to eternal torments."

- Dr. Thomas Guthrie: "My belief is that in the end there will be a vastly larger number saved than we have any conception of. What sort of earthly government would that be where more than half the subjects were in prison? I cannot believe that the government of God will be like that."

- Dean Richard W. Church: "I should be disloyal to Him whom I believe is as the Lord of truth if I doubted that honest seeking should at last find Him here, man's destiny stops not at the grave, and many, we may be sure, will know Him there who did not know Him here."

- Dean A.P. Stanley says that: "In the 'world to come' punishment will be corrective and not final, and will be ordered by the Love and Justice, the height and depth of which it is beyond the narrow thoughts of man to conceive."

- Professor Challis says: "...so that the end of divine punishment is for correction, and for giving effect to the establishing of universal righteousness."

- William Law: "As of the purification of all human nature either in this world or some after ages, I fully believe it." And again, "Every number of destroyed sinners ...must through the all-working, all redeeming love of God, which never ceases, come at last to know that they had lost, and have found again, such a God of love as this." (Read Psa. 103:9; Mic. 7:18; Lam 3:31-33; Isa. 57:16)

- Dr. Lightfoot: "In our English translation the word 'hell' seems to speak what is neither warrantable by Scripture or reason."

- Rabbi Loewe: "*Olam* simply signifies for a long time. The Hebrew Scriptures do not contain any doctrine referring to everlasting punishment."

- Philippson, in his ***Israel Religionslehre***, says (11:255), "The Rabbi teach no eternity of hell torments; even the greatest sinners were punished for generations."

- Charles H. Welch wrote in ***An Alphabetical Analysis***, (vol. 1, p. 279), "Eternity is not a Biblical theme." And (vol. 1, p. 52), "What we have to learn is that the Bible does not speak of eternity. It is not written to tell us of eternity. Such a consideration is entirely outside the scope of revelation." Welch was the editor of ***The Berean Expositor***, and a man well versed in Greek.

- A.E. Knoch wrote in his small booklet ***What are the Facts, Eternal Torment or Universal Reconciliation?*** (page 51), "To sum up: though the Bible and the various views are contradictory on this subject, an accurate inquiry into the grammar, the scope and the application of each text shows us that most of them refer to the process, not the goal; they are temporary, not eternal; they include few, not all, therefore we can believe all that God has said. The last and highest revelation through the apostle Paul stands as it is written, that ALL mankind shall be saved (1 Tim. 2:4; 4:10), justified (Rom. 5:18), vivified (1 Cor. 15:22), and the universe (Col. 1:20) in heaven as well as on earth, will be reconciled with God through the blood of His cross." Mr. Knoch worked with the Hebrew and Greek texts for more than fifty years. He is the author of so many articles concerning the Scriptures that his writings make a complete library. While our versions in common use vary where the English translation of the words "eon" and "eonian" occur in relation to "punishment;" nevertheless, where universal reconciliation is in view, all are translated similarly, including the KJV. (See Rom. 5:18-19; 8:18-25; 11:25-36; Eph. 1:9-11; 3:11; Phil. 2:10-11; Col. 1:15-20; 1 Tim. 2:3-6; 4:9-11; Heb. 2:9; 1 John 2:2; Rev. 4:11.)

Those who see and believe the truth of universal salvation as the purpose of God's plan for the eons, or ages, say those verses in some versions which are translated so they teach endless punishment have been incorrectly translated; yet no one seems to suggest that the verses which teach universal reconciliation have been. It would seem that many of the "translators" were simply commenting upon what they believe, rather than translating what the Greek and Hebrew convey. The work of a translator is to literally and faithfully bring over into another language what the text of the Greek and Hebrew say, and to let the commentators make of it what they will.

Paul told Timothy (2 Tim. 3:16) that "all Scripture is inspired by God and is beneficial for teaching, for exposure, for correction, for discipline in righteousness, that the man of God may be equipped, fitted out for every good act." Each word in the whole of the Scriptures was carefully chosen by God that He might reveal to mankind His plan and purpose for it. Jesus spoke of the importance of even the smallest letter of the law (Matt. 5:18). Paul's instruction to Timothy emphasized the importance of having a "pattern of sound words which you hear from me" (2 Tim. 1:13). The writers of the Hebrew and Greek Scriptures were inspired to write exactly what God told them to write.

Unfortunately, no translator was so inspired. One cannot see the truth of the word *aion* as it is translated in our common version without the aid of a knowledge of the Greek and Hebrew themselves, or without some study aid, such as a concordance, lexicon, or a faithful literal translation or other such help. Such versions as Rotherham's ***Emphasized Version***, or the ***American Standard Version*** with marginal notes, are of help, as are the concordances previously mentioned, to those who do not know the languages of inspiration.

Chapter Thirteen

Punishment?-Yes -- Everlasting?-No

"He saves all, but converting some by punishment, and others who follow by their own will-that every knee may bend to Him, of things in heaven and earth and under the earth."
-St. Clemens of Alexandria

"As of the purification of all human nature either in this world or some after ages, I fully believe it."
-William Law

Let us consider some of those passages used to refute universal salvation. Jesus, speaking to the Jews, said, "I go My way and ye shall seek Me, and shall die in your sins; where I go, ye cannot come" (John 8:21). This has been used in argument and in sermons as a verse to attempt to show some will go into eternal punishment. But Jesus was telling those to whom he spoke that He would be returning to His Father, but they could not go with Him there. He also used the words "ye cannot come" when He spoke to His *believing* disciples (John 13:33-36). In neither case was he speaking of their final disposition.

At John 3:36: "He that believeth on the son hath everlasting life; and he that believeth not on the Son shall not see life, but the wrath of God abideth on him." Here Jesus is speaking of *eonian* life, not *eternal* life. As shown previously, there are those who will not enjoy the life of the two eons following the present one, but they will be raised at the consummation of the eons, reconciled to God, and He to them, as a result of the white throne judgment. Again, Jesus was not speaking of their final state.

Some refer to the "eternal damnation" of the KJV as proof of eternal punishment. The Greek words *apollumi* and *krino*, correctly translated, mean: *appolumi*, "destroy," "lose" (in the active voice) and "perish" or "be lost" (in the passive); *krino*, "judge" (in the active voice), and "am being judged" (in the passive). The noun derived from *apollumi*, *apoleia,* means "destruction" or "waste." But this word was translated "damnation" at 2 Peter 2:3 in the KJV, and "damnable" at 2 Peter 2:1. *Apoleia* is used in the Textus Receptus Text in Acts 25:16. This is the text supposedly used by the King James translators. However, the truth of the matter, is that the Greek text used by the King's translators differed with the so-called Textus Receptus in at least 287 places. (See *Facts on the Textus Receptus and the King James Version* by Dr. Allan A. MacRae and Dr. Robert C. Newman, Biblical School of Theology, Hatfield, Pa.) They translated *apoleia* "die." It is obvious that any man the Romans delivered to "die" *apoleia,* will be resurrected and judged. (See John 5:28,29; Acts 24:15) Therefore, *apeleia* cannot mean "no future life," it cannot mean the ultimate annihilation of any man. *Krino*, the word for "judge" occurs 14 times, and is once rendered damned (2 Thes. 2:12). The noun derived from it, "judgment," occurs 24 times and in seven of these occurrences was translated "damnation," yet in 13 instances in the same version it was translated "judgment." *Krisis*, another form derived from the verb, and meaning "judging," occurs 49 times in the Greek text. The translators of the KJV rendered it "judgment" 41 of those times, "condemnation" 3 times, "damnation" 3 times, and "accusation" twice. All those judged are not condemned nor are they damned. Judging involves setting affairs right between two parties in a suit, deciding an issue, coming to a conclusion. The English words "damn," "damnation," and "damned" have no equivalent in the Greek text, and should not have been used as the translation of any word appearing there. There is a compound of the word for "judge," *katakrino*, "condemn" which occurs 24 times in the N.T. Twice the KJV translated it "be damned." To condemn means to judge adversely, but again, the final state is not in view where the word appears in the text.

Perhaps the best summary against the use of the word "damn" and its derivatives in the Bible come from the pen of F.W. Farrar, a Canon of the Church of England. He writes in his *Mercy and Judgment on page 369*:

"The words 'damn' and its derivatives do no once occur in the Old Testament. In the New Testament they are the exceptional and arbitrary translation of two Greek verbs or their derivatives which occur 308 times. These words are 'appolumi' and 'krino.' 'Apolleia' (destruction or waste) is once rendered 'damnation' and once 'damnable.' (2 Peter 2:3, and 2 Peter 2:1); 'krino,' (judge) occurs 114 times, and is only once rendered 'damned.' (2 Thess. 2:12) 'Krima,' (judgment or sentence) occurs 24 times, and is 7 times rendered 'damnation.' 'Katakrino,' (I condemn) occurs 24 times, and is twice only rendered 'be damned.'

Now turn to a modern dictionary, and you will see 'damnation' defined as 'exclusion from divine mercy; condemnation to eternal punishment.'

But to say that such is the necessary meaning of the words which are rendered by 'damn' and 'damnation,' is to say what is absurdly and even wickedly false. *It is to say that a widow who marries again must be damned to endless torments (1 Tim. 5:12, 'having damnation,' krima), although St. Paul expressly recommends young widows to do so two verses later on. It is to say that everyone who ever eats the Lord's Supper unworthily, eats and drinks "eternal punishment' to himself, though St. Paul adds, almost in the next verse, that the judgment (krima) is disciplinary and educational to save us from condemnation. (1 Cor. 11:29-34) It is to say that 'the Day of Judgment' ought to be called 'Day of Damnation' (John 5:29) It is curious that our translators have chosen this most unfortunate variation of 'damn' and its cognates only fifteen times out of upwards of two hundred times that krino and its cognates occur; and that they have it for 'krisis' and 'krima,' not for the stronger compounds 'katakrima,' etc. The translators, however, may not be to blame. It is probable that 'damn' was once a milder word than 'condemn,' and had a far milder meaning than that which modern eschatology has furnished to modern blasphemy. We find from an Act passed when a John Russell was Chancellor (in the reign of Richard III or Henry VII), that the sanction of an Act against extorted benevolences is called 'a damnation' - that is, 'the infliction of a loss.' This is the true* *etymological meaning of the word, as derived from damnum, 'a loss'; and this original meaning is still found in such words as 'damnify,' 'indemnify,' and 'indemnity.' In the margin of 1 Cor. 11:29, we find 'judgment' for 'damnation'; whereas in verse 32 the 'judgment' of the Lord is milder than His 'condemnation.' Dr. Hey, in his lecture on the Ninth Article, says that the phrase, 'it deserveth God's wrath and damnation,' is used in the milder sense of the word which was originally prevalent. However this may be, the word has, as the Bishop of Chester says, undergone a modification of meaning from the lapse of time, and it is an unmixed gain both it and its congeners will wholly disappear from the revised version of the English Bible. 'Judgment' and 'condemnation' are the true representatives of 'krisis' and 'katakrisis,' and they are not steeped, like the word 'damnation,' in a mass of associated conceptions which do not naturally or properly belong to them. Equally unfortunate is the word 'hell.'"*

The above writing was penned before the first major revision of the King James Bible was printed. His words came true. The Revision of the KJV removed the "damn" words from the pages of the Word bringing us a few steps closer to removing the tarnish the church has put upon the character of the Creator of all human beings.

Another argument against Universalism is Matthew 7:13,14. *"Enter ye in at the strait gate: for wide is the gate, and broad is the way, that leadeth to destruction, and many there be with go in thereat: because strait is the gate, and narrow is the way, which leadeth unto life, and few there be that find it."* (King James Version)

This passage must be interpreted according to its context. The context of the Gospels is the kingdom in which Jesus will be reigning on this earth. Matthew 7:13,14 is in the context of the Sermon on the Mount. This sermon presents the principles and the rule of Jesus in His Kingdom on this earth. *"Blessed are the meek: for they shall inherit the earth."* (Matt. 5:5) This passage tells us the real nature of this sermon, for the meek have never inherited the earth nor have they ever reigned. It is important that we do not confuse events which will happen here in earth in future ages with what happens in eternity. Generally, revelation about events far into the future are not revealed by God until it is time.

(Editor's note): Unfortunately, the doomsday preachers of all generations have made this mistake over and over again. Tertullian, a leading third century theologian who, unfortunately gave us many of our theological words that we never seem to be able to understand, was certain Jesus was going to come in his life-time and set up his kingdom. They were even certain where it would begin and it was not Jerusalem. He and the rest of the Montanist sect were obviously wrong. Martin Luther stated he was certain the world would end within 50 years. Martin Luther was wrong. There are dozens of denominations of Christianity that were founded by people who were certain enough of when Jesus would return that they set exact dates. They were wrong, but many of the denominations which were formed based on their false dates are still with us.

The entrance way into the fullness of the Life Jesus Christ desires for us to have **is** certainly strait and narrow. There is room for only one person to pass through and that is Jesus Christ Himself. No one apart from being crucified with Him an becoming one with Him will enter into this realm. Our pastors, elders, Popes cannot stand besides us. There is room for only one. Our traditions, creeds, "correct" doctrines cannot come with us. There is only One Word. There is room for only Him. Our prejudices, anger, bitterness, self-righteousness, self-pity etc., cannot come with us. There is only room for Love. While millions of Christians think that their denomination is the way ...that is why they are it, they are greatly mistaken, and are on the road that leads to destruction, that is, they will suffer great loss. That is what that word translated "destruction" means. We will have to let go of our denominational titles to get in. We will have to let go of our self-righteousness which came from our theology, our traditions, our heritage, our "correct" keeping of His laws. All that will have to go. The list is endless of the things we will have to let go of which actually keeps us from experiencing the fullness of His Life. The carnal Christian will suffer great loss when facing The Door Who is the door. It is truly best to let go of these things now. Then we may enter into that *aionion zoen* right here on earth.

While it is outside the focus of this paper, I want to make a brief comment on the subject of aionion life, translated by the King James translators "eternal life." In the 16th Chapter of John's Gospel verses 32 and 33, Jesus leaves some departing words for his disciples. He said,

"Indeed the hour is coming, yes, has now come, that you will be scattered, each to his own, and will leave Me alone. And yet I am not alone, because the Father is with Me. These things I have spoken to you, that in Me you my have peace. In the world you will have tribulation; but be of good cheer, I have overcome the world." Jesus spoke these words, lifted up His eyes to heaven, and said: "Father, the hour has come. Glorify Your Son, that the Son also may glorify You, as You have given Him authority over all flesh, that He should give eternal life to as many as You have given Him. And this is eternal life, that they may know You, the only true God, and Jesus Christ whom You have sent." So then *aionion zoen*, incorrectly translated "eternal life" is knowing God, the Father, and Jesus Christ, His Son. How well do you know God, the Father and His Son? The Bible tells us that to be carnally minded is death. (Rom. 8:6) The Scriptures say we can grieve and quench the Holy Spirit. They tell us our traditions can make the word of God of none effect. (Matt. 15:6; Mark 7:13) They tell us that the "Kingdom of God" **is** "righteous, peace, and joy." (Rom. 14:17)

Unfortunately, for most Christians too much of their "relationship" or "knowing" God, the Father and His Son, Jesus Christ is nothing more than memorizing the Scriptures and believing their church traditions. "Knowing" someone is not the same as knowing the Scriptures or church traditions about Jesus. There is a real intimacy which we can enter with God even while here on earth. This intimacy varies with each individual, and it varies from day to day within a believer's life. To be carnally-minded cuts off the flow of *aionion zoen*. Does that mean we have lost our place in heaven after this life? Of course not! But the quality of our Christian life here on earth is at jeopardy. "Righteousness, peace, and joy" as words are nothing more than words. But the reality of those words when we truly abide in Him are beyond words, nevertheless, very real. *Aionion Zoen*, translated by some of the more accurate translations with "age-lasting life" "age-during life," "life of the ages," or "eonion life" emphasize that Jesus is not only interested in redeeming everything lost, but those who have been brought into the kingdom in this dispensation, should taste and experience some of the reality of His life right now! It should manifest! We should be able to get to know more and more each day the reality of Him because we have a relationship with Him beyond words on a page in a Bible. The mistranslation of the word aionion to "eternal" has robbed millions of Christians of the fact that God wants us to experience His life now. Most Christians think of "eternal life" as something we get after we die. This is sad, because as a result of this concept, we are not manifesting a quality of life that we should presently be walking in. "Righteousness" is not just being moral. His peace far exceeds being calm during tough times. And His joy leaves the "happiness" the world lusts for, far behind. The fruit of the Spirit unfortunately for many Christians are empty words memorized in a Bible study. A proper understanding of "aionion zoen" will restore to us a key to "knowing" Jesus Christ, the Savior of the Whole World and His Father. The reality of this "life" which He gave us, will speak much more to the inhabitants of this world than words "about" Jesus. (End of editor's note)

Chapter Fourteen

A Long, But Not Eternal Visit To "Hell"

"In our English translation the word 'hell' seems to speak what is neither warrantable by Scripture or reason."
-Dr. Lightfoot

"'Olam' (the Hebrew for aion) simply signifies for a long time. The Hebrew Scriptures do no contain any doctrine to everlasting punishment."
-Rabbi Loewe

"The writers of Hebrew and Greek Scriptures were inspired to write exactly what God told them to write. Unfortunately, no translator was so inspired."

When I tell church members about God's victorious love and grace, that God through Christ Jesus "*will draw all men*" (John 12:32); "*all men to justification of life*" (Rom. 5:18,19); "*in Christ shall all be made alive*" (1 Cor. 15:22-28); "*to head up all in the Christ*" (Eph. 1:10); "*That in the name of Jesus every knee shall bow...every tongue should be acclaiming that Jesus Christ is Lord, for the glory of God*" (Phil. 2:10,11); "*Who will have all men to be saved*" (1 Tim. 2:4); "*We have our hope set on the living God Who is the Savior of all men*" (1 Tim. 4:10); "*The all is created through Him and for Him*" and "*Through Him to reconcile the all to Him (making peace through the blood of His cross*" (Col. 1:16, 20). When I declare God's glorious plan to restore all back to Himself, church members ask, "But what about hell?"

Jesus never used the English word "hell" and He never used any Greek, Hebrew, or Aramaic word meaning what most people believe "hell" means. For years I have asked preachers, "How many times is the word "hell" in the Bible, and how many Hebrew and Greek words are translated "hell" in your King James Bible?" None of them answered the question. Therefore, I will now present for the reader a summary of the original Hebrew and Greek words which the King James' translators rendered into the English word "hell." The transliterated spelling of these words comes from *Young's Analytical Concordance to the Bible.*

The only Hebrew word translated "hell" in what is commonly called the Old Testament, is the word "Sheol." "Sheol" occurs 65 times. It is translated "hell" 31 times, "grave" 31 times, and "pit" 3 times in the King James Bible. It is obvious that if "Sheol" means "hell," it should not be translated "grave." "Sheol" means the same as the Greek noun "Hades."

"Hades" is derived from the Greek verb "horao." "Horao" means "I am seeing." The Greeks then prefixed the word with "a" (alpha) which negates "to see" thus coining the noun "Hades" meaning "unseen." Therefore, "Sheol" and "Hades" mean "unseen." These two words do not describe what the English theological word "hell" means to convey. That the King James translators did not understand what "Sheol" and "Hades" meant is proved by the following:

"*Out of the belly of hell (Sheol) cried I.*" (Jonah 2:2) Verse 1:17 tells us he was "*in the belly of the fish for three days and three nights.*" Where was Jonah - in Hell or in a fish? If "Sheol" is translated "unseen" we have no problem. Jonah was in the "*belly of the fish*" and was "unseen." We know that Jonah was "*in the belly of the fish for three days and three nights.*" (Jonah 1:17) This agrees with the words of Jesus, for He said, "*For as Jonah was three days and three nights in the belly of the great fish.*" (Matt. 12:40) In the Greek Septuagint, (the Hebrew Old Testament translated into Greek around 200 B.C.) we find the Greek adjective *aionios* translated "forever" in Jonah 2:6 in the King James Bible. It is obvious that *aionios* "forever" cannot mean more than three days and three nights. There is a problem here.

In 1 Cor. 15:55, the King James' Greek text contains the Greek word "Hades." They translated the Greek word "Hades" into the English word "grave," but they gave an alternative translation "Hell" in the margin. In Rev. 20:13,14, the Greek Text contains the word "Hades" which they translated into the English word "Hell." In the margin they put the alternative translation of "grave." It should begin to appear to the objective reader of the King James Bible that the translators were uncertain as to the meaning of the words "Hades" and "Sheol." The modern reader of a King James Bible printed in this century will not know this because many of the modern editions of the KJV have removed the marginal readings the original King James contained. Does something smell a little foul here?

"Hades" occurs 11 times in the King's Greek Text (often misnamed "Textus Receptus"). When we study "Hades," let us remember that according to the KJV, Jesus was in "Hell." (see Acts 2:27, 31) Obviously Jesus' soul was not in "hell-fire."

Another Greek word "Gehenna" occurs 12 times in the New Testament; 11 times in the Gospels and one time in the Epistle of James. Jesus used "Gehenna" about 7 times. Some of the occurrences of "Gehenna" are in parallel passages, that is, they refer to the same event. "Gehenna" is the Greek form of the Hebrew "ge-hinnom." It literally means "valley of Hinnom." Sometimes it is referred to as the "valley of the sons of Hinnom." In the Old Testament "Tophet(h)" also refers to this place. (See Young's Concordance under Hinnom) "Gehenna" is a valley that lays on the west and southwest of Jerusalem. In the valley, Israel offered up its children as a burnt offering to a god who came to be known as Moloch. (The spelling varies)

(Editor's note: Knowing there would be many questions about the Greek and Hebrew words incorrectly translated "Hell," we felt it appropriate to give a few more details to answer some of those questions. There are entire books just on these words. We certainly do not have the space in this work to answer all questions, but hopefully we have included enough material to let the reader see that there are reasonable Scriptural, historical, and scholarly support for our conclusions. The next few pages have been added to Mr. Abbott's work with his permission.)

In Jeremiah, we hear Yahweh speaking to Jeremiah regarding this sacrifice, "*And they have turned to Me the back, and not the face; though I taught them, rising up early and teaching them, yet they have not listened to receive instruction. but they set their abominations in the house which is called by My name, to defile it. And they built the high places of Baal which are in the Valley of the Son of Hinnom, to cause their sons and daughters to pass through the fire to Molech, which I did not command, nor did it come into My mind that they should do this abomination, to cause Judah to sin.*" (Jer. 32:33-35) Jeremiah says this valley would one day be called the "Valley of Slaughter." (Jer. 7:30-33) This Scripture had its literal fulfillment in 70 A.D. at the destruction of Jerusalem.

King Josiah, in his days, desecrated this place by tearing down all the idols, crushing or burning them, and burning human bones on them (probably those of the priests who presided over these rituals). A Jew was not allowed to touch anything that touched a dead human being. Please note, it was God's own people who were doing the burning, not God, and He said such a thing never entered His mind. Also note, not one single time in the entire Old Testament was this word "Ge-hinnom" translated "hell."

In Jesus' day, this valley was a city dump very much like modern dumps-always being filled, and therefore always having something for the fire to consume and worms to eat. ("*where the worm dieth not, and the fire is not quenched.)* It was a place fit only for waste. Should a Jew, God's "chosen" people ever be given a burial in "Gehenna," it would be the most humiliating thing that could ever happen to him. It would be like saying that one's life here on earth was completely worthless, fit only for the dump. For Jesus to tell a religious Jew, such as a Pharisee, that his life, his religious works, his devotion to God were fit only for the city dump, was to insult him in the worst possible way. Jews went to great efforts to make their funerals great events. Some even hired professional "mourners" to cry at their funeral. Herod was going to have the leaders of Israel killed on his day of death so that Israel would mourn on his death. This is the kind of mentality Jews had regarding their life and they way they should leave this world. Even today, one will hear Jews say that the most important thing a person owns is his name. They will go to great lengths to keep their name alive. They will name buildings, start foundations, etc., to keep their name alive. Many, who no longer believe in a resurrection feel this is the only way they can stay alive beyond the grave - to have their name remain in the minds of future generations.

Returning to "Gehenna," one can walk through this valley even today and return unscathed by its fires and untouched by the worms which actually consumed a good part of the religious Priestly community of Israel in the destruction of Jerusalem in 70 A.D. Their bodies were piled up and their blood ran down into this very valley which Jesus prophesied would be the disgraceful burial place for hundreds of thousands of Jews of that very generation Jesus was speaking to. Please remember, it was not the heathen, not the street sinner, not the Roman who found themselves in this "hell" as the KJV wants to render it - it was God's own people - even more - it was those who thought they were closer to God than anyone else on the earth. Beware, Christian, that you do not find yourself committing the same mistake!

Whatever this valley represented in the Old Testament must be carried over to the New Testament. Nowhere in the Old Testament is this place translated "Hell" and nowhere in the Old Testament is there a hint that this place referred to a place of eternal punishment after death. The word which Jesus referred to most often which the King James Bible unfortunately chose to render "hell," in the New Testament, but *did not do so in the Old Testament*, is this word "Hinnom" or Ge-hinnom (valley of Hinnom) or "Ge-ben-hinnom" (valley of the sons of Hinnom) which was transliterated into the Greek as "gehenna." A thorough study of this place in the Old Testament will dispel much myth regarding its significance. The Scriptural references for such a study are: Josh. 15:8; 18:16; 2 Kings 9:7; 15:3,4; 23:10, 36, 39; Ez. 23:37,39; 2 Chr. 28:3; Lev. 18:21; 20:2; Jer. 7:30-32; 19:2-6; 32:35. Remember, this place is *never* referred to as "Hell" in the Old Testament. References to this very same place in the New Testament are: Matt. 5:22; 5:29, 30; 10:28; 18:9; 23:15; 23:33; Mark 9:43; 9:45; 9:47; Luke 12:5; James 3:6. It should be mentioned that most of these references come from Jesus' mouth and every reference to this word "gehenna" was addressed to God's own people, not to the nations around Israel.

The Greek word “tartarus” occurs one single time in the entire Bible and it is found in 2 Peter 2:4. It is the place where sinning messengers (angels) are reserved unto judgment. The English word "Hell" occurs 54 times in the King James Bible, and is a translation of 4 Hebrew and Greek words. Not one of the words has a meaning even closely related to the meaning theologians have given the English word "Hell." Many Bibles translated in the last one hundred years do not contain the English word "Hell." Almost all of them have found no justification for translating "Sheol" into "Hell." Therefore, almost all English Bibles do not contain any references to our modern concept of "Hell" in the Old Testament. From Genesis to Malachi, "Hell" has disappeared as a result of better translating. Many Bibles have eliminated the word entirely and the day will come when all Bibles will no longer teach this pagan concept which should never have been in our translations in the first place.

The King James translators were honest enough to admit in their "To the Reader" found in the original printings of the King James Bible that they built upon other men's work and that others would build up theirs. They did not claim inerrancy nor infallibility. Their many marginal readings proves that. Unfortunately, most modern King James Bible printings have removed that letter as well as the marginal readings. Why? Well, modern Fundamentalists and many Evangelicals have created a doctrine entitled "The Doctrine of Biblical Inerrancy." Since the letter reveals that the translators did not believe they were writing an "inerrant" translation and the alternative readings in the margins would substantiate that, these connivers have removed the letter "To the readers" and the marginal readings to hide this fact. An example of the kind of marginal readings these "inerrancy" advocates have removed: the marginal reading of Luke 17:36 read, "*This 36th verse is wanting in most of the Greek copies.*" They weren't sure of the original Greek for this verse and let the reader know. This kind of honesty is impermissible in the "inerrancy" camp.

The "Doctrine of Inerrancy" is a myth of the most diabolical kind perpetrated by religious leaders seeking to keep God's people in darkness. The King James Bible today will differ from the one printed in the year 1611 in thousands of places. From one publisher to another there will be differences in the KJV.

Returning back to the subject of "Hell," we have found that the Hebrew word "Sheol" should never have been translated "Hell." The Jews today, whose Bible consists of the Old Testament do not translate it "Hell" because in no way does "Sheol" correspond with the images and doctrines the church associates with the word "Hell." The Greek word "Hades" is the equivalent of "Sheol" and has the same meaning.

The Greek mythological place the Greeks called "Tartarus" occurs one time in the Biblical text to denote a holding place for messengers (angels) "til" judgment which indicates an eventual release from this place. The case against "Gehenna" being translated into "Hell" is very aptly summarized by Dr. J.W. Hanson in his *The Bible Hell* when he listed the following regarding "Gehenna" :

1. *Gehenna* was a well-known locality near Jerusalem, and ought no more to be translated *Hell*, than should Sodom or Gomorrah. See Josh. 15:8; 2 Kings 17:10; 2 Chron. 28:3; Jer. 7:31,32; 19:2.

2. *Gehenna* is never employed in the Old Testament to mean anything else than the place with which every Jew was familiar.

3. The word should have been left untranslated as it is in some versions, and it would not be misunderstood. It was not misunderstood by the Jews to whom Jesus addressed it. Walter Balfour well says: 'What meaning would the Jews, who were familiar with this word, and knew it to signify the valley of Hinnom, be likely to attach to it when they heard it used by our Lord? Would they contrary to all former usage, transfer its meaning from a place with whose locality and history they had been familiar from their infancy, to a place of misery in another world? By what rule of interpretation, then, can we arrive at the conclusion that this word means a place of misery after death?

4. The French Bible, the Emphatic Diaglott, Improved Version, Wakefield's Translation, and Newcomb's, retain the proper noun, *Gehenna*, the name of a place as well-known as Babylon. (Many other Bibles since this was written, have also removed "Hell" and put "Gehenna" back.

5. *Gehenna* is never mentioned in the Apocrypha as a place of future punishment, as it would have been, had such been its meaning before and at the time of Christ.

6. No Jewish writer, such as Josephus, or Philo, ever used it as the name of a place of future punishment, as they would have done had such then been its meaning.

7. No classical Greek author ever alludes to it, and therefore, it was a Jewish locality, purely.

8. The first Jewish writer who ever names it as a place of future punishment is Jonathan Ben Uzziel, who wrote, according to various authorities, from somewhere between the second to the eighth century A.D.

9. The first Christian writer who calls *Hell, Gehenna,* is Justin Martyr, who wrote about A.D. 150.

10. Neither Christ nor his apostles ever named it to Gentiles, but only to Jews, which proves it a locality only known to Jews, whereas, if it were a place of punishment after death for sinners, it would have been preached to Gentiles as well as to Jews.

11. It was only referred to twelve times, on eight occasions, in all the ministry of Christ and the apostles, and in the Gospels and Epistles. Were they faithful to their mission to say no more than this, on so vital a theme as an endless *Hell*, if they intended to teach it?

12. Only Jesus and James ever named it. Neither Paul, John, Peter, nor Jude ever employ it. Would they not have warned sinners concerning it, if there were a *Gehenna* of torment after death?

13. Paul says he 'shunned not to declare the whole counsel of God,' and yet, though he was the great preacher of the Gospel to the Gentiles he never told them that *Gehenna* is a place of after-death punishment.

14. Dr. Thayer (author of *Thayer's Lexicon* and also on the translation committee to the *American Standard Bible*) significantly remarks: 'The Savior and James are the only persons in all the New Testament who use the word. John the Baptist, who preached to the most wicked of men, did not use it once. Paul, wrote 14 epistles, and yet never once mentions it. Peter does not name it, nor Jude; and John, who wrote the gospel, three epistles, and the Book of Revelation, never employs it in a single instance. (the Greek words of "lake of fire" in Revelation is not *Gehenna*) Now if *Gehenna* or *Hell* really reveals the terrible fact of endless woe, how can we account for this strange silence? How is it possible, if they knew its meaning, and believed it a part of Christ's teaching, that they should not have used it a hundred or a thousand times, instead of never using it at all; especially when we consider the infinite interests involved? The Book of Acts contains the record of the apostolic preaching, and the history of the first planting of the church among the Jews and Gentiles, and embraces a period of thirty years from the ascension of Christ. In all this history, in all this preaching of the apostles of Jesus, there is no mention of *Gehenna.* In thirty years of missionary effort, these men of God, addressing people of all characters and nations, never, under any circumstances, threaten them with the torments of *Gehenna*, or allude to it in the most distant manner! In the face of such a fact as this, can any man believe that *Gehenna* signifies endless punishment, and that this is a part of divine revelation, a part of the Gospel message to the world? These considerations show how impossible it is to establish the doctrine in review on the word *Gehenna.* All the facts are against the supposition that the term was used by Christ or his disciples in the sense of endless punishment. There is not the least hint of any such

meaning attached to it, nor the slightest preparatory notice that any such new revelation was to be looked for in this old familiar word.

15. Jesus never uttered it to unbelieving Jews, nor to anybody but his disciples, but twice (Matt. 23:15-33) during his entire ministry, nor but four times in all. If it were the final abode of unhappy millions, would not his warnings abound with exhortations to avoid it?

16. Jesus never warned unbelievers against it but once in all his ministry, (Matt. 23:33) and he immediately explained it as about to come in this life.

17. If *Gehenna* is the name of *Hell* then men's bodies are burned there, and well as their souls. (Matt. 5:29; 18:9)

18. If it be the name of endless torment, then literal fire is the sinner's punishment. (Mark 9:43-48)

19. *Gehenna* is never said to be of endless duration, nor spoken of as destined to last forever, so that even admitting the popular ideas of its existence after death, it gives no support to the idea of endless torment.

20. Clement, a Universalist, (of the early church) used *Gehenna* to describe his ideas of punishment. He was one of the earliest of the Christian Fathers. The word did not then denote endless punishment.

21. A shameful death, or a severe punishment, in this life, was, at the time of Christ, denominated *Gehenna,* (Schleusner, Canon Farrar, and others), and there is no evidence that *Gehenna* meant anything else, at the time of Christ." (end of insert from *The Bible Hell)*

Note: While all this historical and etymological information is very helpful, I am sure it will raise many questions which cannot fully be dealt with in such a short work. However, to show the reader how easy it is to answer some of these answers, I will deal with a couple of what many feel are the most troublesome. The reader should write to us for further works on this most important subject. We have many volumes which deal with this subject very thoroughly.

"*Jesus says that the fire of Gehenna is "unquenchable" and one in which God can 'destroy the body and the soul.' That does not sound like a fire of a 'city dump.'"*
As we go through some of these passages, I cannot over stress that fact that Jesus did not utter these words at the local bar, or house of prostitution. He did not go to Rome, Babylon, or Athens and utter these strong warnings. He boldly declared these warnings to God's own people soon to be called for a season "not God's people." (see Hosea 1:9; 2:23; Rom. 9:25)

The physical fires of "Gehenna" have long since gone out. Therefore theologians conclude that these fires must refer to spiritual things. This is called "adding to the word." In one sense, they are correct, that is, the stigma associated with the horrible way the nation of Israel was destroyed, the humiliation of being called "Christ-killers" would stay with the name "Jew" throughout the centuries, even to this day. While the physical fires and worms have passed, the humiliation, the hatred, the torment and abuse which comes with the name "Jew" has remained to this day. Remember the Holocaust, only one generation ago? But this stigma will not last into eternity. The label of "not my people" will not be carried into kingdom of God. So while there is a higher meaning and significance to "Gehenna" than the physical destruction of Jerusalem, it is *not* a symbol of "eternal torment." The shame and persecution will one day be removed.

The Greek word behind the English word "unquenchable" is the word "asbestos." This word has been brought over into the English language describing a substance. Examples of how the word was used in Greek should prove that this word did not define a "fire that would never go out."

"Strabo calls the lamp in the Parthenon, and Plutarch call the sacred fire of a temple "unquenchable," though they were extinguished ages ago. Josephus says the fire on the altar of the temple at Jerusalem was "always unquenchable" (asbestos aei), though the fire had gone out and the temple was destroyed at the time of his writing. Eusebius says that certain martyrs of Alexandria 'were burned in unquenchable fire,' though it was extinguished in the course of an hour."

The above examples should prove the word in the original Greek did not mean a fire that would burn forever. It meant a fire that could not be put out until it consumed that which it was burning. The purpose of the fire on the alter in Jerusalem ended in 70 A.D. when the types and shadows of the rituals in the Law of Moses were replaced by the true light - Jesus Christ, the Light from above and His body of believers who Jesus called the "light of the world."

As to "Gehenna" being a place where God can destroy the "body and the soul," it should be noted that God could also "raise up children to Abraham from these stones," but He didn't. (Luke 3:8) He is able to blot a person out of the Book of Life, but that doesn't mean He will. We must be careful not to add to His Word what is not there.
Jesus' warnings were extremely strong about the fires of "Gehenna." Again, speaking to the "chosen" people,

"*And if thy right eye offend thee, pluck it out, and cast it from thee; for it is profitable for thee that one of thy members should perish, and not that thy whole body should be cast into Hell (Gehenna). And if thy right eye offend thee, cut it off, and cast it from thee; for it is profitable for thee that one of thy members should perish, and not that thy whole body should be cast into Hell.*" (Matt. 5:28,29; see also Matt. 18:9 and Mark 9:43,49)
If these Scriptures are to be taken literally, and if the consequences are eternal torment, then the church should be full of one-eyed, one-armed, one-footed members. The pulpits should have chairs behind them for the multitude of one-footed preachers who have

problems with lustful eyes and hearts, and greed never being satisfied with the amount of money they raise.

I met a Christian who took these Scriptures literally and tried to take out one of his eyes. How many preachers would dare be bold enough in their so-called "faith" to counsel such a man that he was doing the right thing because he was following Scriptures? The justice systems would have those preachers behind bars in no time. Can you see the hypocrisy in this kind of reasoning? If Jesus meant what he said and if the consequences were what preachers tell us they are, then they should teach it *all* from a literal point of view, but they don't. They don't believe their own teachings.

Jesus rebuked God's "chosen people" evangelists declaring they were making their converts "two times the sons of Hell (Gehenna) as yourselves." (Matt. 23:15) If eternal torment is what is implied here, then God has a serious problem. He chose them to be His "evangelists." From the very beginning of Israel's history, God told them that they would forsake Him and become rebellious. (Joshua 23:16 and many other prophesies) If God knew that Israel was going to misrepresent God to the nations, that they would accept false God's and images and make their converts two times the sons of Hell (Gehenna) as themselves, then God is ultimately responsible for the fate of the peoples of this world because He knew in advance that Israel would misrepresent the Truth. If "Gehenna" is eternal torment, God has indicted Himself in being an accomplice to making the world full of people who are "two times the sons of Hell." God Himself chose these people as a nation of priests to the world. It was their responsibility to show the world His standards. They miserably failed. But God knew they would fail before they even began. Therefore, since He had foreknowledge of this fact, He is directly responsible for the world being deceived by His own priests. The buck stops at the top. If eternal torment is the punishment for not living up to God's standards, then God will ultimately have to be blamed for those who are in "Hell." When one studies the church record as being a standard of righteousness and truth in the world, we have even a worse example than Israel. The church, for a long time in its history, forbid people even owning a Bible at the penalty of death! Study church history from a non-denominational point of view and one will see liars, hypocrites, fornicators, murders, covetous, whoremongers, incest, false doctrines, power hungry leaders, Christians killing Christians etc. How can a human being make a reasonable decision regarding the truth when presented with such a miserable example of righteousness and holiness? Ultimately God will have to take the blame if "Hell" is full of "two-times the sons of 'Hell.'" His own evangelists made them that way.

"*The kingdom of God is come nigh unto you. But into whatsoever city ye enter, and they receive you not, go your ways out into the street of the same, and say, 'Even the very dust of your city, which cleaveth on us, we do wipe off against you: not withstanding be ye sure of this, that the kingdom of God is come nigh unto you.' But I say unto you, that it shall be more tolerable in that day for Sodom, than for that city. Woe unto thee, Chorazin! woe unto thee, Bethsaida! for if the mighty works had been done in Tyre and Sidon, which have been done in you, they had a great while ago repented, sitting in sackcloth and ashes. But it shall be more tolerable for Tyre and Sidon at the judgment, than for you. And thou, Capernaum, which art exalted to heaven, shalt be thrust down to hell."* (Luke 10:9-15)

This portion of Scripture will reveal how distorted the Bible becomes when literalists refuse to acknowledge that the Hebrew language is a rich one full of idiomatic expressions. It also reveals some major differences between God's judgments and much of the modern churches concept of judgment. The Greek word behind the word "hell" is this passage is the word "hades" meaning "the unseen." Almost every translation since the KJV of 1611 has eliminated the word "hell" in this passage and substituted the word "Hades" or "the depths," (NEB) or "the dead," (Goodspeed) or "realm of death" (NAB). Even the *New* King James Bible, in the KJV tradition, has abandoned "hell" for "Hades," the unseen.

Most English Bible translations have abandoned "hell" in this passage because there is obviously a problem here if one takes this passage literally. When was an entire city (Capernaum) ever in literal heaven? It never was! And neither will it ever be in the "Hell" of our modern theologians. But Capernaum did experience "heaven" in the idiomatic language of Hebrew *and* Capernaum also experienced the Biblical experience of the meaning of the Greek word "Hades."

Capernaum means "village of Nahum." The Book of Nahum is a short prophetic book which contains a strong prophesy against the city of Ninevah, capitol of Assyria. It prophesied its utter destruction. Capernaum was abandoned in the Islamic invasion in 638 A.D. No one knew the exact location of the city until Tell Hum was excavated in 1968. In what way was Capernaum ever in "heaven?" Looking into a Concordance and studying all the Scriptural references relating to Capernaum will bring forth great understanding. I will only touch the surface here.

If you recall, after His temptation in the wilderness, Jesus went to Galilee. Either the first city, or at least among the first cities He visited was Capernaum. Prior to entering the city, he preached outside the city. Many people from as far a Sidon and Tyre came to hear Him. Sidon and Tyre were not part of Israel, they were pagan cities! Visiting Capernaum was a fulfillment of Isaiah 9:1,2 declaring a light to the Gentiles. (Matt. 4:13-17) It was here Jesus began to preach the Kingdom of God. It was here He healed the Centurion, a non-Jew and said of the Centurion, "I have not found such great faith, not even in Israel!" It was here Jesus said, "But the sons of the kingdom will be cast out into outer darkness. There will be weeping and gnashing of teeth." (Matt. 8:5-13) It was here Peter, the apostle of the Circumcision lived. It was here Jesus said, "Come to Me, all you who labor and are heavy ladened, and I will give you rest." (Matt. 11:28) It was here He preached the principles of the kingdom. (Matt. Chapter 18 and other references) It was here the demons declared in public who Jesus was and He cast them out. (Mark 1:21-36) Being the home of Peter the apostle, who apparently had a large house, Jesus spent a great deal of time in this city. It was in this city that many of the things Jesus did and the words He spoke which were recorded in our Bibles were spoken. It was here the disciples disputed among themselves who was the greatest. (A pastime still in favor among God's present people) (Mark 9:33,34) It was here He raised the dead. (Luke 7:1-

17) It was here Jesus said, "Do not labor for the food which perishes, but for the food which endures to everlasting (aionios) life, which the Son of Man will give to you, because God the Father has set His seal on Him." (John 6:26,27)

Is it too difficult to see that Capernaum was indeed a very privileged, an honored, an exalted, no - even further - a city in which the very kingdom of God on earth was not only declared, but manifested!? What a glorious privilege! It was indeed in "heavenly places" without being lifted up to some place millions of miles away with golden streets! In the same manner, when Capernaum was covered up by the sands of Galilee's seashore after the Moslem's took over the region, can we not see the word "Hades" (unseen because it was covered up, forgotten, and abandoned) perfectly describes the condition of Capernaum after 638 A.D.? Does this city have to go to a physical fiery eternal place to fulfill Jesus' words?

Most Bible translations have abandoned their attempts to maintain modern Christianity' concept of "Hell" regarding Capernaum because they see it doesn't work very well. One day, they will discover, the modern concept of "Hell" doesn't work in any part of the Bible because this pagan myth doesn't exist.

Which brings us to the English word "Hell" itself. Just a little study into the etymology of this word should throw up a warning flag. But Christians are really not taught to study past their own denominational doctrines, and therefore remain "in outer darkness!"

The Origin of "Hell"

It is always amazing to me how much knowledge we have of ancient times. It seems God, in His wisdom, tucked bits and pieces of information aside in the forms of an inscription, a piece of papyrus, a ruin, etc., and man, with his God-given abilities, has been gathering together in recent years these bits of ancient knowledge and reconstructing the past. The study of word origins (etymology) is a very developed science few Christians spend any time studying. If one were to take the main theological words used in church and study their origins, one would learn much.

Remember, the Greek word "Hades" literally meant unseen. The pagans then turned a perfectly good usable word into the name of a God named "Hades" and created a place of the underworld called "Hades." They turned an everyday word with easy to understand meaning into a theological pagan word which, if one studies the "underworld" mythology of the Greeks, into a mass of confusion.

The English word "Hell" suffered the same unslaught, but not from pagan Greeks, but from pagan Christians! According to *Arcade Dictionary of Word Origins* by John Ayto, the etymology of the word "hell" is as follows:

hell (OE) Etymologically, "hell" is a 'hidden place.' It goes back ultimately to Indo-European 'kel' (cover, hide), which has contributed an extraordinary number of words to English, including 'apocalypse," cell,' 'cellar,' 'conceal,' 'helmet,' 'hull,' 'pod,' 'occult,' and possibly 'color' and 'holster.' Its Germanic descendant was 'khel-,' 'khal-,' whose derivatives included 'khallo' and 'khaljo.' The first became modern English 'hall,' the second modern English 'hell-'-so both hall and hell were originally 'concealed or covered places,' although very different ways: the 'hall' with a roof, 'hell' with at least six feet of earth. Related Germanic forms include German 'Holle' (O with an umlaut), Dutch 'hel,' and Swedish 'helvete' (in which 'vete' means punishment').

Isn't it rather interesting that the place where people met under a roof and therefore "covered," (hall) and the place where people are "six feet under" and therefore "unseen," come from the same word? A church and a graveyard therefore have much in common. This book will not go into other theological words such as the word "church," but I assure you, there are many embarrassing surprises hidden in theological word origins.
We have found then, that the modern English word "Hell" was originally not a specific region for those eternally damned, as theologians would term it, but a common everyday word which basically meant "covered up" and therefore often "unseen." This word was useful to describe a number of different things.

But as with "Hades," and "Gehenna," a superstitious religious priestcraft used these normal everyday words and concocted images to hold people in their power. They used their deceptive power-hungry minds to tell the ignorant what was in the "unseen" place of the grave (hell).

They created a goddess in charge of affairs in "hell." She was called "Hel." The hole in the ground became a huge underground empire of which she was ruler. The word with a little "h" became a place with a capital "H."

This information I am bringing forth is not hidden away in some ancient monastery. It can be found in almost any book on word origins, regular dictionaries, and encyclopedias. But when Christians have been taught to stick their heads into a "hole" or "hall" called our "church building" and not to look at anything which does not conform to "their" teachings, it leaves most Christians in "gross darkness" - in other words in a "hell" of their own.

Even excellent study Bibles such as the Companion Bible by Dr. E.E. Bullinger, perhaps the best KJV Study Bible available, brings out the fact that these words have been greatly tampered with by the priestcraft. Under his appendage number 131 *The synonymous words for "Hell", etc.* he states:

"The English word is from the Anglo-Saxon 'hel', Genitive Case 'helle'=a hidden place, from the Anglo-Saxon 'helan'=to hide."

Dr. Bullinger covers the others words we have just been discussing. His appendages bring great light into a darkness many Christians have been placed into, allowing themselves to be "covered" by false shepherds.

A quick tour through the Norse and Germanic mythologies of the goddess Hel and her domain Hell should be a wake up call to any person whose mind is still functioning. The Encyclopedia Britannica tells us of "Hel":

"*Hel or Hela, in Scandinavian mythology, goddess of the dead, a child of Loki and the giantess Angurboga, dwelt beneath the roots of the sacred ash, Yggdrasil (q.v.), and ruled the nine worlds of Helheim. In early myth all the dead went to her: in later legend only those who died of old age or sickness; she then became synonymous with suffering and horror.*" It is common knowledge to anyone who has studied church history even just a little bit, that the Roman Catholic church made it a practice to absorb the pagan traditions of the nations which it tried to covert. She, the Roman Catholic church, by the power she claimed, just Christianized them. From this practice, we Christians have inherited all the superstitions of the world. Under the word "Hell" they incorporated the mythologies of the Romans, Greeks, Babylonians, Egyptians, Teutons, Druids, and only God knows what else.

This work cannot go into the thousands of pagan words, myths, rituals, artifacts, originating in pagan religions which have been brought into the Christian religion. Reading Hislop's *Two Babylons*, published by Loizeaux Brothers, or *Babylonian Mystery Religion* by Ralph Woodrow would be two good places to begin. For those of the Protestant persuasion who think they are immuned to the influence of Romanism, think again, the entire Protestant Sunday morning church ritual, including the structure of the building and its interior furniture, will not be found among the early believers in Jesus Christ.

While the Scriptures correctly translated have nothing to say about the modern theological concept of "Hell," nor do they speak of "eternal punishment," they do have much to say about "judgment."
-end of editor's note.

Those who believe in "hell" as a place of punishment (although the two words *never* appear together in the Scriptures, even in mistranslations) do not seem to remember the verse which says Jesus' soul was in "hell" three days and three nights. For what was He being punished? In the KJV at 1 Cor. 15:55, the word translated "grave" in the text is changed to "hell" in the margin, and at Rev. 20:14-15, the word "hell" in the text is changed to "grave" in the marginal reading! Apparently the translators could not make up their minds which word should be used. The word in the text used by the translators of the KJV is *hades*, meaning "unseen." It means neither "grave" nor "hell."

The evangel, or gospel, contained GOOD NEWS, for that is the meaning of the Greek word *euaggelion*, good news "which shall be to ALL people" (Luke 2:10). There is little "good news" in condemning the majority of humanity to eternal damnation, or punishment and saving just a few. It is noticeable that those who are so eager to condemn others to "hell" eternally do not include themselves, their families, or their friends in such a fate. Most, however, object to the idea that God loves ALL of mankind. Instead, they believe God loves only those whom He calls, but not the sinners.

Chapter Fifteen

The "Chosen" -- Not "I have chosen"

"Many today are like the Jews we read about in the book of Acts, who were jealous, and believed God loved them alone, and who were boasting in their works."

Paul tells us in his writings at Rom. 9:1-5 of his great sorrow, and that he wished himself to be anathema from Christ for the sake of his brethren, the unbelieving Israelites, but there are those who believe most of mankind is "lost eternally" who do not show such concern. These good people do not have the sorrow Paul expressed. O' that they might know that all we have, our faith, our salvation, and our calling come only through the grace of God and the faith of His Son Jesus Christ! It is not through our own works, but through God's working in us that we have this marvelous grace (Eph. 2:8-10; Phil. 2:13; Rom. 8:28-31; 1 Cor. 1:26-31; 4:7; Heb. 12:2).

Many today are like the Jews we read about in the book of Acts, who were jealous, and believed God loved them alone, and who were boasting in their works. We must not be like the man who said he had accepted Christ, that he chose to believe the gospel, hence he was saved, but those who would not accept Christ were lost and on their way to hell. Our Lord said (John 15:16), "*Ye have not chosen Me, but I have chosen you.*" Romans 8:29 says: "*...whom He foreknew, He designates beforehand, also, to be conformed to the image of His Son. Now whom he designated beforehand, these He calls, these He justifies also; now who He justifies, these He glorifies.*" And Ephesians 1:4 says, "*...according as He chooses us in Him before the disruption of the world...in love designating us beforehand for the place of a son for Him through Christ Jesus.*" Jesus said (John 12:31-41) of those who did not believe He would be exalted out of the earth and would be drawing ALL to Himself that "they could not believe," seeing that *God* "hath blinded their eyes and calloused their heart." But again, this condition was not to last eternally, as verse 32 shows. We should be boasting in Christ Jesus (Rom. 15:17) and the faith of Jesus (Rom. 3:26) rather than in our own works.

1 John 4:8 tells us: "God is love," and 1 John 2:2 that "He is the propitiation for our sins and not for ours only but also for the sins of the whole world;" 1 John 4:11, "God so loved us," and John 3:16, that "God so loved the world that He gave His only begotten Son," that is Christ, Who (Heb. 2:9) "by the grace of God tasted death for EVERY man." Revelation 4:11 says of Him, "Thou art worthy, O Lord, to receive glory and honor and power, for Thou hast created ALL things, and for THY pleasure they are and were created." Is there pleasure to be gained in knowing beforehand that those who were created would never hear the GOOD NEWS of the gospel, would never believe and would be sent to "hell" forever to be tormented? All this for His pleasure? If we are instructed to love our enemies (Matt. 5:44) can we expect God to do less?

Chapter Sixteen

Clearing Things Up

"I am convinced that God loves all, (John 3:16, Rom. 5:6-10), and that 'love never faileth.' (1 Cor. 13) Therefore, if one sinner is endlessly lost, that sinner has defeated the LOVE of God and that is impossible."

In Dr. W.E. Vine's ***Dictionary of New Testament Words*** there appears under the subject "Ever, For Ever, Evermore, Everlasting" (vol. 2, pp. 46-47), "The following phrases are formed in connection with *aion*, an age: They are idiomatic expressions betokening undefined periods and are not to be translated literally." He follows by listing several instances in which the word occurs, and gives a literal and accurate translation. Yet he calls these "idiomatic expressions!" All languages have idiomatic usages for words, that is true, but we must not consign literal statements to idiomatic meanings. Paul tells us we must have a pattern of sound words, which we hear from him (2 Tim. 1:13). Using the translating of "forever and ever" instead of the "age of the age," or "ages of the ages," or "age of the ages," as the case may be at such places as Eph. 3:21, Heb. 1:8, or Gal. 1:5, as Dr. Vine does, saying they are not to be taken literally, is not using a pattern of sound words. Why are they not to be taken literally? They certainly are understandable when so done. Dr. Vine also says that (p. 47) "**Everlasting**. *Aionias* should always be translated 'eternal' and *aidios* 'everlasting.'" To translate 2 Tim. 1:9 and Tit. 1:2 with what he calls "idiomatic" words of the English is the only way to make sense out of them. To use "forever" or "forever and ever" there makes nonsense.

Sometimes the KJV translates another word, *aidios*, "imperceptible," with the word "everlasting." The Greek word appears twice in the Scriptures, once at Jude 6 and again at Rom. 1:20. Literally translated, the verse in Jude should be: "Besides, the messengers who keep not their sovereignty but leave their own habitation, He has kept in imperceptible bonds under gloom for the judging of the great day." (CV) Yet the KJV says: "*The angels which kept not their first estate, but left their own habitation, he hath reserved in everlasting chains under darkness unto the judgment of the great day.*" The "everlasting" in this case is only "unto" the time of their judging. Dr. Vine evidently believes the common teaching of the denominational groups, rather than what his own knowledge of the Greek should have revealed to him, had he not considered this to have been "idiomatic" usage.

We must remember that while God's words are inspired and refined as though put through a crucible seven times, men's translations of those words are not inspired. But with translations such as the ***Concordant Version***, ***Rotherham's Emphasized Version***, the ***American Standard Version*** (with marginal notes) and others, and by using such aids as lexicons and concordances of the Hebrew and Greek, we will be able to regain the truth concerning the eons, or ages, spoken of in the Scriptures.

To continue with the Scriptures used to refute universal salvation, let us look at John 3:36: "*He that believeth in the Son hath everlasting life; and he that believeth not the Son shall not see life, but the wrath of God abideth on him.*" There was a time when all of us were unbelievers and were without a knowledge of Christ, but when we became believers, and came to be in Christ, we received life. Can we say this Scripture teaches that those who die in their sins will never see life, or will never be resurrected? Revelation 20:15 says they will, as do John 5:25-30; Acts 24:15, 21; 26:8 and the fifteenth chapter of 1 Corinthians. John 3:36 is speaking of not seeing "eonian life," or "life of the ages," not "eternal life."

- ***The Emphasized Bible*** (Rotherham) translates the verse, "*He that believes on the Son hath life age-abiding; whereas he that yieldeth not unto the Son shall not see life, but the anger of God awaiteth him.*"

- ***The Emphatic Diaglott*** (Wilson): "*He believing into the Son has aionian life; but he disobeying the Son shall not see life, but the anger of God abides on him.*"

- ***Young's Literal Translation***: "*He who is believing in the Son hath life age-during; and he who is not believing the Son shall not see life, but the wrath of God doth remain on him.*"

- ***Concordant Version***: "*He who is believing into the Son has eonian life, yet he who is stubborn as to the Son, shall not be seeing life, but the indignation of God is remaining on him.*"

The Greek word *menei*, a 3 person singular, present active indicative form from *meno*, means "remaining," or "abiding," and has no meaning of endlessness. Should it have meant so, then our Lord would still be abiding wherever He was when those came to question him, as recorded in John 1:38, for the same word is found in that verse, and was translated "dwellest" in the KJV.

That the Scriptures declare an end to God's anger should dispel the notion that God's wrath will abide upon a mass of people "forever and ever." Psa. 103:9 says: "He will not always chide, neither will he keep His anger forever." His anger is "age-abiding," "age-during," or "eonian," not "forever." Even leaving the incorrect "forever" in this text proves an end to God's wrath.

Believers in Christ have eonian life, life through the ages. The ones not believing will not see that life, but will be raised, judged and sent into death a second time. The second death of Rev. 20:14 and 21:8 is not endless, for Paul tells us in 1 Cor. 15:26 that death will be destroyed. "Therefore, we both labor and suffer reproach, because we trust in the living God, Who is the Savior of ALL mankind, specially of those who believe." (1 Tim. 4:10) God is the Savior of ALL, but in this eon He is offering a special salvation, that of life throughout the eons, to those who believe. At the end of the eons, the remainder of mankind will also be made alive in Christ. Those who believe that have no difficulty with John 3:36.

Second Thessalonians 1:9 says (KJV), "*Who shall be punished with everlasting destruction from the presence of the Lord...*" The Greek text says, *olethron aionion*, "eonian extermination." The word does not imply extermination beyond recovery, for it is limited to the eons by the adjective modifying it. The word is used at 1 Cor. 5:5, where it is recorded that Paul delivered "*such a one unto Satan for the destruction of the flesh, that the spirit may be saved in the day of the Lord Jesus.*" There is no word in all of Scripture which even suggests annihilation, eternal destruction, loss or death from which there is no recovery, or a condition from which salvation is impossible. Always such terms as "destruction," "perish," "be lost," and "death," are relative to a period of time during an eon or during the eons.

The fire the KJV says "never shall be quenched" (Mark 9:43-44) and "where the worm dieth not" are regarded by some as the most terrifying of all found in the Scriptures. To many this verse is "proof" for the endlessness of "hell-fire" (Matt. 3:12; Luke 3:17; Mark 9:43-46,48). But of what was the Lord speaking? The word "worm" is correctly translated here, as well as at Isa. 66:24 and Jonah 4:2. It in no way can be construed to mean it destroys the spirit, for that returns to God upon death (Ecc. 12:7; Luke 23:46; Acts 7:57). Neither can it destroy the soul, for it can be destroyed in Gehenna (Matt. 10:28). Rather, the thought expressed here is that just as worms feed upon partly decayed flesh, they will feed upon the unburned portions of the bodies of the dead who are cast into Gehenna during the millennial eon when some fail to observe the kingdom code. Those will not be allowed to continue, lest they contaminate the kingdom. But notice also that it is never said that any living being will be cast into Gehenna.

The word "unquenchable" occurs four times in the N.T. (Matt. 3:12; Luke 3:17; Mark 9:43, 45). An unquenchable fire is one which is not put out, but continues to burn until all is consumed. In the past God brought unquenchable fire against Jerusalem and other places (Jer. 4:3,4; 7:16-20; 21:11,12, and Eze. 20:45-49). Those fires are not burning today. Those who are cast into Gehenna will be suffering their first death, and that for specific acts of wickedness. Some will pass directly into the kingdom from this eon without dying first. This was the secret Jesus revealed to Martha, as recorded at John 11:26. But those who are cast into Gehenna will be raised after the thousand-year reign of Christ, at the time of the white throne judgment, and will be judged and requited for their deeds. Then all whose names are not found in the book of life will suffer a second death (Rev. 20:1-5; Rom. 2:1-16), after which they will be raised at the consummation of the eons, when death will have been destroyed, and ALL will have been reconciled to God. The judgment of Gehenna has nothing to do with the final state, nor are its consequences endless, nor of eternal duration.

Another common argument against Universal Reconciliation is the case of Judas. Advocates of everlasting punishment quote the KJV, Mark 14:21, "The Son of Man indeed goeth, as it is written of him : but woe to that man by whom the son of Man is betrayed! Good were it for that man if he had never been born." The first question which must be settled is whether Jesus uttered these words as translated in the KJV. As the last clause in this verse is used in opposition to Universal Reconciliation, let us look carefully at the Greek text: *kalon en auto eiouk egennethe ho anthropos ekeinos*, "Ideal were it for Him if that man were not born" or "It were ideal for Him if that man was not born." The question is asked, Who is the Him? The answer is in the preceding clause. There we have the pronoun *autou*, "Him," and *anthropo ekeino*, "that man," both referred to in such a way that we cannot mistake them. "The Son of Man indeed goeth as it is written of Him; but woe to that man by whom the Son of Man is betrayed!" "Him" is the Son of Man, "that man" is Judas. The Him cannot refer to Judas, therefore the text can be paraphrased as, "Ideal were it for Him (the Son of Man) if that man (Judas) were not born."

Notice how the following versions translates this clause: The ASV, 1901 margin, "Good were it for him if that man had not been born;" Rotherham's version, "Well for him if that man had not been born;" Murphy's edition of the Douay Version and the New Testament translated from the Latin Vulgate, 1898, "It were better for him, if that man had not been born;" (the following three versions are quoted in the original spelling) Wiclif, 1380, "It were good to hym if thilke man hadde not been borun;" Tyndale, 1534, "Good were it for him if that man had never bene borne;" Rheims, 1582, "it were good for him, if that man had not been borne." Therefore, Mark 14:21 does not contradict Col. 1:15-20; 1 Tim. 4:9-11; Rom. 5:18, 19; etc., all teaching the ultimate salvation of Judas. John Albert Bengel in his New Testament Word Studies, vol. 1, p. 290, says about this clause, "This phrase does not necessarily imply the interminable eternal of perdition." Dr. Bengal was a German Lutheran theologian.

When I quote the KJV in 1 Tim. 4:9, 10, "This is a faithful saying worthy of all acceptation. For therefore we both labour and suffer reproach because we trust in the living God, who is the Saviour of all men, specially of those that believe," I have been challenged. My opponents say, "'Specially' means God is the Saviour only of those who are now believers, therefore God is not the 'Saviour of all men.'" Let us look at this word "specially" as it is used by Paul. The Greek word is *malista.* The word *malista,* "specially," is a superlative preference adverb meaning above all, particularly, chiefly, most, specially, especially. Let us look at two other scriptures where Paul uses this adverb. Galatians 6:10: "As we have therefore opportunity, let us do good unto all men, especially unto them who are of the household of faith." Brethren, my question is: "Is the doing of good unto all men or is it limited to the household of faith?" 2 Timothy 4:13, "The cloak that I left at Troas with Carpus, when thou comest, bring with thee, and the books, but especially the parchments." Were Paul's instructions in 2 Tim. 4:13 limited to the parchments? Surely it is obvious from these two examples that this adverb *malista,* "specially," cannot be used to limit the "all men" in 1 Tim. 4:10. In these few examples that have been quoted herein as they are used in opposition to God's ultimate purpose to save all mankind, I have given a scriptural answer proving the truth of universal reconciliation. Now, I am sure that all the arguments of the opponents can be answered by the Scriptures. I am convinced that God loves all, (John 3:16; Rom. 5:6-10); and that "love never faileth," (1 Cor. 13). Therefore if one sinner is endlessly lost, that sinner has defeated the LOVE of God and that is impossible.

Chapter Seventeen

The Complete Revelation

---

1 Corinthians 15:22-28
"The more one studies this Scripture as well as dozens like it, it becomes abundantly clear that as in Adam ***all*** *died, the very same* ***all*** *will be made alive in Christ. There is not one in Adam who will not be made alive in Christ."* - Louis Abbott

"Paul, in 1 Corinthians 15:22-28 takes us much farther into the future than does the book of Revelation."

Some say that the teaching of universal salvation, or reconciliation, gives one license to do as he wishes with no fear for the consequences, and the "hell-fire" must be taught in order to keep them in line and get them saved. Some say also that Paul's teaching of salvation by grace gives license to sin, but consider this fact: Denominational teaching has included threats of eternal punishment in hell for many centuries, and it has not "saved" the masses of humanity as yet. Do men serve God best when they realize He loves humanity, or when they fear He will send them to "hell" forever? Romans 5:8-12 tells us God loved us while we were yet sinners, and sent Christ to die for the sake of the irreverent. Although most seem to believe the book of Revelation tells of God's ultimate goal, Paul tells us it was given to him to complete the words of God and the consummation was revealed to him, not to John, even though in human measurement of time, Revelation probably was written after the books attributed to Paul. Paul says (Col. 1:25), "...of which I became the dispenser according to the administration of God, which was given to me for you, to complete the word of God." He was not speaking in terms of time, but in matters of revelation. It is through the writings of Paul that we get the truths concerning God's ultimate goal for mankind, as well as for the entire universe.

Dr. J.B. Lightfoot, in his commentary on Colossians, says (p. 67), "The word *plerosai*, to fulfill; i.e., to preach fully. To give its complete development to." Luther used *reichlich predigen*, "to preach fully," and Olshausen says: "That is, to declare the gospel in all its fullness and extent." Each of these writers were commenting upon the *plêrosai*, the completing of the revelation of God, by Paul.

Mr. Ray A. Van Dyke, compiled a comparison between the revelation given in Revelation and that given to Paul, as recorded in 1 Cor. 15:22-28. His comments are reproduced here: "In the book of Revelation we do not have the final plan of God. Paul, in 1 Cor. 15:22-28 takes us much further into the future than does the book of Revelation. To illustrate this more clearly, study the following: 1 Cor. 15:22-28 as compared with the new heaven and new earth of Revelation 20:21-22:

In 1 Cor. 15:22-28, we have:

- No more rule
- No more authority
- No more power
- No more enemies
- No more reigning
- All subjected
- No more death, death destroyed.
- All made alive, immortal

In Revelation 20:21-22, we have:

- Still rule (20:6; 22:5)
- Son still reigns (22:1-5; 11:5)
- Authority (21:24,25)
- Power (21:24,25; 22:2
- Kings (21:24-26)
- Saints reign (22:5)
- Second death still exists (21:5)
- The nations still mortal (22:2)

-end quote

Christians who believe in universal reconciliation believe that the Bible is God's Word, and His Word cannot contradict itself, hence the inspired sacred Scriptures say in Rev. 11:15; 22:5, *eis tous aionas ton aionon*, "for the eons of the eons." Thus, Christ our Lord "reigns for the eons of the eons," not as the king's translators rendered, "forever and ever." Therefore, Revelation 20:21, 22 fits into the framework of the eons, and is truth relative to the eons. First Corinthians Chapter 15 fits at the consummation (end) of the eons. We give the second Adam, Christ, as much credit and numerical ability as the first Adam, and use 1 Cor. 15:22-28 also for this truth. (Read Rom. 5:18-19.)

Consequently, Col. 1:16-20:

All in heaven and earth created in Him (verse 16)

All for Him (verse 16)

All estranged are reconciled (verse 20)

1 Corinthians 15:22:

In Adam all are dying

In Christ shall all be made alive

The literal Greek in 1 Corinthians 15:22 reads:
hosphor gar en to Adam pantes apothneskousin houtos kai en to christo pantes zoopoiethesontai.

"Even as for in the Adam all are dying, thus also in the Christ, all shall be made alive."

The more one studies this Scripture as well as dozens more like it, it becomes abundantly clear that as in Adam all died, that very same all will be made alive in Christ. There is not one in Adam that will not be made alive in Christ. It is a perfectly balanced statement which Jesus said was already set in motion. "And I, if I be lifted up from the earth, will draw (drag in Greek) all mankind unto Myself. (John 12:32, NKJV)

Your Part

Now that you have read this book, it's your turn.

If the truths presented here have helped you, don't let these truths die in your hands.

Please write to us and let us know your thoughts concerning its content.

Consider assisting us in getting this book into the hands of those who would be encouraged and strengthened by its message:

- Recommend it to your friends and loved ones.
- Order additional copies to give as gifts.
- Keep extra copies on hand to loan to others.

If you have not read the author's other works, order them today.

We would be honored to have your fellowship in getting this book freely to those who hunger spiritually. We have daily opportunities to send it to pastors, Sunday school teachers, Bible college professors and students, Bible class teachers, and prisoners.

Daily Email Goodies™

Do you receive our

Daily Email Goodies™?

These are free daily emails that contain short quotes, articles, and studies on Biblical themes.

These are the original writings of Clyde L. Pilkington, Jr, as well as gleanings from other authors.

Here is what our readers are saying:

"Profound! Comforting! Calming! Wonderful!" – NC

"The Daily Email Goodies continue to bless my heart! ... They provide plenty of food for thought." – IL

"I really appreciate the Goodies!" – VA

"Your Daily Email Goodies are making me aware of authors whose names I don't even know." – GA

"I am glad to be getting the Daily Email Goodies – keep 'em coming." – IN

Request to be added to our free

Daily Email Goodies™

If you would like to be added to the mailing list, email us at:

Goodies@StudyShelf.com